T0306060

Healthcare Workforce Transitioning

Competency Conversations through World Café

Healthcare Workforce Transitioning

Competency Conversations through World Café

Dr. Anne L. Drabczyk

Routledge
Taylor & Francis Group

A PRODUCTIVITY PRESS BOOK

First edition published in 2019
by Routledge/Productivity Press
52 Vanderbilt Avenue, 11th Floor New York, NY 10017
2 Park Square, Milton Park, Abingdon, Oxon OX14 4RN, UK

First issued in paperback 2021

Printed on acid-free paper

ISBN-13: 978-0-367-02403-1 (hbk)
ISBN-13: 978-1-03-209351-2 (pbk)
ISBN-13: 978-0-429-39981-7 (eBook)

Library of Congress Cataloging-in-Publication Data

Names: Drabczyk, Anne, author.
Title: Healthcare workforce transitioning : competency conversations through
World Cafe / Dr. Anne Drabczyk.
Description: Boca Raton : Taylor & Francis, 2019. | Includes bibliographical
references.
Identifiers: LCCN 2018053054 (print) | LCCN 2018058664 (ebook) | ISBN
9780429399817 (e-Book) | ISBN 9780367024031 (hardback : alk. paper)
Subjects: | MESH: Allied Health Occupations--education | Competency-Based
Education--standards
Classification: LCC R697.A4 (ebook) | LCC R697.A4 (print) | NLM W 18 | DDC
610.69--dc23
LC record available at https://lccn.loc.gov/2018053054

This book is dedicated to Daniel and Matthew, in celebration of your respective talents; may you always thrive, and to Toby, eternally my North Star.

Contents

List of Tables xiii

Preface xv

Author xix

1 Healthcare Competencies: Framework for a Program 1

Origin of the Competency Conversation 1

The Institute of Medicine Reports 1

Implications for Healthcare Workforce Transitioning 3

Healthcare Competency Potential 4

Competency Inspired Initiative: Public Health

Accreditation Board 7

Competency Framework for an Academic Program 8

The Better Understanding and Learning Design

(BUILD) Survey 9

BUILD Focus Group 10

BUILD Student Listening Session 12

Development of a Healthcare Degree Matrix 13

Step 1: Selection of Healthcare Management

Competencies 13

Step 2: Determination of Program Learning

Outcomes 14

Step 3: Documentation of Course Identifiers 15

Step 4: Determination of Course Learning

Outcomes 15

Step 5: Development of Course Key Performance
Indicators 15
Step 6: Recommendation of Course Assessment
Methods 16
References 16

2 Professional Development Portfolios.....................19
Career Advancement through Professional
Development Documentation...19
Toward a Meaningful Academic Professional
Development Process..22
Professional Development Service Learning Portfolio 22
Professional Development Service Learning Reports 25
Professional Development Service Learning
Applications..29
Professional Development: Personal Career
Transitioning..32
Professional Development: Advancing the Institution......34
Closing Thoughts 35
References 36

3 World Café 39
World Café Overview..39
Principle 1: Clarify the Purpose and Set the Context 40
Principle 2: Create a Hospitable Space...........................42
Principle 3: Explore Questions That Matter 42
Principle 4: Encourage Everyone's Contribution..........44
Principle 5: Connect Diverse Perspectives 45
Principle 6: Listen Together for Insight 45
Principle 7: Share Collective Discoveries: Debriefing
the Data 45
World Café Host Role..46
World Café Table Host Role...47
Hosting a World Café..50
Inviting Participants..50
Venue and Setting 50
Establishing a World Café Agenda..................................51

World Café Facilitation Steps 52
World Café Debriefing 54
    Student Conversations...54
    Student and Healthcare Professional
    Conversations 57
    PDSL World Café Lessons Learned...........................58
Promising Healthcare-Focused World Café
Applications..59
References 61

4   Healthcare Communication Competency 63
Communication Competency: Impact on Six Aims for
Quality Improvement..63
Communication Competency: PDSL Insights...................66
    Relationship Management...67
    Communication Skills 68
    Facilitation and Negotiation 69
Communication Competency: World Café Debrief..........71
Communication Competency: Promising Practices 74
    REDE Model 74
    Hospital Consumer Assessment of Healthcare
    Providers and Systems 75
Closing Thoughts 77
References 78

5   Healthcare Leadership Competency 79
Leadership Competency: Assuming Accountability..........79
Leadership Competency: PDSL Insights..........................81
    Leadership Skills...81
    Organizational Climate and Culture...........................83
    Communicating Vision.. 84
    Manage Change.. 86
Leadership Competency: World Café Debrief.................. 88
    Values-Driven Leadership Skills................................ 88
    Relating to People 89
    Guiding Organization toward Success 90
Leadership Development: Promising Practices 91

Institute for Healthcare Improvement Open School
for Health Professions 91
Customized Programs 92
Appreciative Inquiry 93
Closing Thoughts 96
References 97

6 Healthcare Professionalism Competency...............99
Beyond Professionalism toward Interprofessionalism 99
Professionalism Competency: PDSL Insights.................. 102
Personal and Professional Accountability.................... 102
Professional Development and Lifelong Learning....... 104
Contributes to the Community and Profession........... 105
Professionalism Competency: World Café Debrief 106
Professionalism Competency: Promising Training
Practices.. 109
Pre-Career Professionalism Training........................... 109
Professionalism through Case Competition 110
Professionalism Training for Personal Care Aides 111
Institutional Values and Professionalism 112
Closing Thoughts 112
References 113

7 Healthcare Environment Competency 115
Healthcare Environment: Mirroring Societal Trends....... 115
Virtual Healthcare 116
Retailing of Healthcare.. 116
Changing Healthcare Workforce.................................. 118
Healthcare Environment Competency: PDSL Insights 119
Patient's Perspective 119
Healthcare Personnel 121
Community and the Environment................................ 123
Healthcare Systems and Organizations 124
Healthcare Environment Competency: World Café
Debrief.. 125
Healthcare Environment Promising Practices 127
Environmental Stewardship 127

Preparedness Planning...................................128
Healthcare Workforce: Reinventing Careers...............129
Closing Thoughts 130
References 131

8 Business Skills Competency 133
Business Skills Competencies: Agile and Adaptable.......133
  Technology 133
  Human Resources 135
Business Skills Competency: PDSL Insights...................137
  Quality Improvement.....................................137
  General Management......................................138
  Risk Management...139
  Financial Management 139
  Human Resources Management 140
  Information Management...............................141
  Strategic Planning and Marketing...............142
  Organizational Dynamics/Governance 143
Business Skills Competency: World Café Debrief..........144
Business Skills: Promising Practices 146
  Focus on the Patient 146
  Innovation 147
  Assessing Employee Values and Strengths.................149
Closing Thoughts 151
References 151

9 Healthcare Workforce Transitioning 153
Competencies and the Healthcare Workforce...............153
  Ability to Apply Competency 153
  Academia's Role...154
  Organizational Roles 156
Fourth Aim: Focus on the Healthcare Workforce..........158
  Job Engagement and Satisfaction................159
  Job Crafting 162
Closing Thoughts: Keeping the Conversation Alive 164
References 165

Index 167

List of Tables

Table 2.1 PDSL Reports: 2016/2017 Academic Year 25

Table 2.2 PDSL Reports: 2017/2018 Academic Year 27

Table 3.1 PDSL World Café Conversation Questions 43

Table 3.2 PDSL World Café Table Host Training Agenda 49

Table 3.3 PDSL World Café Conversation Agenda 52

Table 4.1 World Café Communication Competency
Debrief 72

Table 5.1 World Café Leadership Competency Debrief 89

Table 6.1 World Café Professionalism Competency
Debrief 107

Table 7.1 World Café Healthcare Environment
Competency Debrief..126

Table 8.1 World Café Business Skills Competency
Debrief 145

Preface

The urgency for healthcare reform was made evident by the Institute of Medicine seminal report *To Err Is Human: Building a Safer Health System*. Key proposals for transformation followed shortly in *Crossing the Quality Chasm: A New Health System for the 21st Century*. Next, focus on the healthcare workforce as an instrument to advance necessary change was proposed in *Health Professions Education: A Bridge to Quality*. Against this historic backdrop, the origin of the competency conversation was fostered. Chapter 1 nudges a thought process on linkages between competencies and grooming a healthcare workforce, in as much transition as the healthcare system, and imagining potential in such a vision. The success story of the affiliation between Public Health Competencies and the Public Health Accreditation Movement is shared to demonstrate the competency connection potential. Academia also plays a pivotal role in nurturing this connection, and the chapter concludes with an example of a competency-based framework for an academic program; one that will contribute to a career-ready healthcare workforce.

There is no doubt that ongoing professional development is essential to a successful healthcare management career, whether one is an early careerist, mid-level manager, or executive. Higher education provides an excellent environment to instill this lifelong learning passion into a student's practice, and provides an avenue to accomplish the objective. Chapter 2 explores the journey of one academic program to develop a meaningful co-curricular activity to foster professional development of the healthcare workforce. Students were compelled to explore opportunities where they could gain healthcare experiences in five overarching competencies: communication, leadership, professionalism, knowledge of the healthcare environment, and business skill competencies. Each semester, students would document lessons learned on E-portfolios, and a cumulative report would be made available to students in the subsequent semester. The competency examples in the report provided talking points, case studies, and were meshed with course learning outcomes that appeared to move students toward a more profession-focused outlook. The chapter concludes with suggestions for using healthcare competency-focused portfolios for personal career transitioning and institutional applications.

To expand professional E-portfolios, conversations about competencies were facilitated through World Café, a proven participative method that promotes meaningful conversations. Chapter 3 provides an overview of the seven principles of World Café, essential roles of the World Café host and table host, and a sample agenda is provided, enabling the reader to replicate the experience. Specifics are detailed on how to facilitate a World Café healthcare competency inquiry through both student-centric, and joint-student and healthcare professional conversations. Insights provided by students and healthcare professionals answer the query: *How can healthcare students facilitate Professional Development Service Learning co-curricular experiences in each of the five competencies?* The chapter concludes with examples of how World Café has been adapted and applied by healthcare professionals to advance important healthcare agendas.

Five healthcare competencies are analyzed in Chapters 4 through 8. Competency vignettes are included in each chapter, as drawn from student E-portfolios. Insights on each competency are also examined from World Café debrief sessions.

Chapter 4 examines communication, which appears across a number of competency lists for a reason: it is indispensable in accomplishing the six aims for improvement, vis-à-vis healthcare reform. Now more than ever, it is obvious that the healthcare workforce will have to be competent in all aspects of communication, in order to successfully navigate a system in transition. Improved communication practices can contribute to the national healthcare objective. The chapter concludes with a review of promising practices including the REDE Model, and the Hospital Consumer Assessment of Healthcare Providers and Systems, which can improve communication and patient satisfaction indicators.

The healthcare environment is explored in Chapter 5. The healthcare landscape is rapidly changing and strong leadership accountability is needed to navigate the shift. Key leadership competencies are examined, including communicating a shared vision, organizational climate and culture, and change management. Emerging practices are also explored, such as framing leadership as a process, and not simply a role, and incorporating emotional intelligence practices into a leader's repertoire. Promising healthcare leadership practices include the Five Practices of an Exemplary Leader, a student-centric program, a customized approach to leadership development, and Appreciative Inquiry.

Chapter 6 assesses professionalism through the lens of inter-professionalism, which describes the very environment the healthcare workforce has to navigate in today's healthcare system. Promising practices in professionalism training, academia, and community partnerships are explored. Case competitions provide students with an opportunity to analyze and present a solution to real issues faced by healthcare organizations, and gain professional skills and confidence through the process. Organizations link professionalism with value and mission statements and tie these professional standards to quality of care.

Chapter 7 explores the healthcare environment that mirrors society. Just as civilization is wired through round-the-clock

Internet and instant messaging, so too healthcare has expanded virtual resources such as telemedicine and virtual care. National changes in retail, with an "add to cart" mind-set, have shifted thinking about access to include healthcare at the corner drugstore. Standard healthcare job descriptions such as physician, nurse, and respiratory therapist, now include new titles like patient navigator and community health worker. How the business of healthcare gets accomplished, where, and by whom, represent changes in the healthcare environment. This chapter examines new healthcare trends, perceptions, and responses of healthcare, untethered from the traditional medical setting. Promising practices in environmental stewardship, preparedness planning, and career trends are also reviewed.

Chapter 8 delves into how technology is driving the way in which business is being conducted. In order to keep pace, today's health employee will have to hone business skill competencies that are agile and adaptable. The connected workforce has to adapt to artificial intelligence, and simultaneously keep an eye on cybersecurity. Emerging titles like Chief Innovation Officer signal both a need and response for organizational agility. This chapter concludes with analysis of promising business practices that focus on patient storytelling and strength-based value assessments for employees.

Chapter 9 explores avenues for the healthcare workforce to apply competencies, and the responsibility both academia and healthcare organizations have in this endeavor. The Fourth Aim is examined as an interesting concept that shines the light on the connection between meeting the Triple Aim, through acknowledgment of the role of the workforce. Job engagement and satisfaction and job crafting are covered as key components of personnel sustainability. The chapter concludes with an invitation to keep the conversation about the healthcare workforce in transition alive, with healthcare competencies as a coalescing beacon.

Author

Anne L. Drabczyk, PhD, is Program Director and faculty for the Healthcare Management Program at Indian River State College on Florida's Treasure Coast. Dr. Drabczyk has over 40 years of healthcare leadership experience, and earned a doctorate degree in Public Health from Walden University in Minneapolis, Minnesota. She holds both a master's degree in Health Administration and a bachelor's degree in Community Health Education and Psychology from Central Michigan University in Mt. Pleasant, Michigan. She is certified in the Appreciative Inquiry Positive Business and Social Change protocol from the Weatherhead School of Management at Case Western Reserve University in Cleveland, Ohio.

In former positions, Dr. Drabczyk was the National Program Director for the Advanced Practice Center for Public Health Preparedness at the National Association of County and City Health Officials in Washington, DC. She was Principal Investigator for The Ohio State University College of Public Health, Center for Public Health Practice, where she liaised with the State of Ohio Department of Health to develop and execute strategic preparedness initiatives. Dr. Drabczyk has been a consultant for several clients in the public health enterprise, and Interim CEO, directing reorganization of a national healthcare association. With over 22 years as an adjunct faculty and consultant for the National Emergency Training Center/National Fire Academy, Dr. Drabczyk specialized in course development and teaching in community risk reduction, resiliency, and leadership.

Dr. Drabczyk lives in Stuart, Florida with her husband Toby.

Chapter 1

Healthcare Competencies: Framework for a Program

Origin of the Competency Conversation

Advancing healthcare workforce transitioning is not a new idea. For the last couple of decades it has been a component of healthcare reform. Indeed, the healthcare workforce is in as much transition as the healthcare system. In order for the restructuring agenda to progress, we must support a focus on the very personnel and teams that will make an optimal healthcare system a reality. One component of such a focus rests with sustaining a healthcare competencies conversation, and we will examine the origin of that dialogue.

The Institute of Medicine Reports

In order to give context to this chapter, a little history will be helpful. The Institute of Medicine seminal report,

To Err Is Human: Building a Safer Health System, revealed
the shocking state of healthcare in the United States, and
focused on the need for patient safety and reduction of
errors (Institute of Medicine 1999). The foundational report
was followed by *Crossing the Quality Chasm: A New Health
System for the 21st Century*, and highlighted "what we
know to be good quality healthcare and what the system
actually provides." The *Chasm* report set forth "an ambitious
agenda redesign of the broken health care system to achieve
six national quality aims; safety, effectiveness, patient-
centeredness, timeliness, efficiency, and equity" (Institute of
Medicine 2001).

The emerging healthcare paradigm is going to be a
challenging goal, and of particular interest is the need to
prepare the workforce. As stated in the *Chasm* report:
"therefore, the importance of adequately preparing the
workforce to make a smooth transition into a thoroughly
revamped healthcare system cannot be underestimated"
(Institute of Medicine 2001). To meet this objective would
require a redesign of the way health professionals are trained
to emphasize the six aims for improvement.

The next major publication, *Health Professions Education:
A Bridge to Quality* concentrated on the healthcare workforce.
The recommendation of the report was that "all health
professionals should be educated to deliver patient-centered
care as members of an interdisciplinary team, emphasizing
evidence-based practice, quality improvement approaches, and
informatics" (Institute of Medicine 2003b).

The foundational work of the Institute of Medicine occurred
long before the Patient Protection and Affordable Care Act of
2010, which added many more previously uninsured Americans
to an already burdened system, and so the conversation about
competency is indeed timely. One example of how healthcare
is experiencing a paradigm shift is as fundamental as how
business is conducted, moving from a fee-for-service approach
to a value-based one. "In value-based models, healthcare

providers are paid on the basis of keeping healthy patients healthy while caring for and improving the health of those suffering from acute and chronic illnesses with cost-effective and evidence-based treatments" (Lipstein et al. 2016, p. 6).

A burgeoning patient pool and major system changes underscore just how timely a healthcare reform conversation really is. Thompson (2018) noted "in the last quarter, for the first time in history, healthcare surpassed manufacturing and retail, the most significant job engines of the 20th century, to become the largest source of jobs in the U.S. The entire healthcare sector is projected to account for a third of all new employment."

Implications for Healthcare Workforce Transitioning

Certainly it stands to sense that as the healthcare system is under scrutiny to change, so too there are implications for the healthcare workforce in transition. Healthcare News (2018) reported "a low supply of healthcare workers is quickly becoming the biggest challenge to meeting patient care demand. This challenge is exacerbated by other important issues, such as changing reimbursement formulas, increasing competition, complex regulatory mandates, technology demands, and uncertain and disparate public policies." If the healthcare workforce resource is left undeveloped, the repercussions could literally mean the difference between life and death.

A survey of healthcare executives identified core competencies of a successful healthcare executive of the future. "These competencies include management skills across hospitals, ancillary providers, physician practices, ambulatory settings, as well as skills and risk management and quality. Results suggested how the curricula of healthcare administration programs can be revamped" (Love and Ayadi 2015, p. 4). The American Hospital Association website details *Bridging Worlds; the Future Role of the Health Care Strategist*

(2017), and "the report is a comprehensive roadmap for skill development, self-assessments, and targeted educational activities to grow individual and team skill sets." Emphasis on multidisciplinary teams seems to be a model for tackling healthcare reform challenges.

The healthcare field is dynamic and changing now more than ever. To keep pace with healthcare reform will require a skilled workforce that can transition as the system does. The healthcare worker of today and tomorrow will have to have a broad array of competencies in their arsenal to successfully manage patient-centered and evidence-based practice, all while being a member of an interdisciplinary team. It is apparent that America's top thought leaders are concerned and focused on the healthcare workforce. Exploring the potential that healthcare competencies offer in preparing the workforce of the 21st century is one way to ensure a career-ready workforce up for the task.

Healthcare Competency Potential

The case for healthcare reform was brought into sharp focus by groundbreaking Institute of Medicine reporting, and the urgency to train a 21st century healthcare workforce has been acknowledged. Perhaps the current phase of this journey toward an optimal healthcare system is embracing the potential of healthcare competencies. If our path forward is made possible through the workforce in transition, then connecting competency with performance to improve systems may just be our guiding light.

Given the complexity of healthcare disciplines, it is understandable that a varied list of competencies would ascend throughout the system. So, what are the essential skills germane to healthcare? Many associations and agencies have attempted to answer this question.

The Healthcare Leadership Alliance (HLA), an association of leading healthcare member organizations defined competencies as "clusters that transcend unique organizational settings and are applicable across the environment" (Stefl 2008, p. 360). HLA identified five core competencies: communication and relationship management, professionalism, leadership, knowledge of healthcare systems, and business skills and knowledge.

Englander et al. (2013, p. 1090) conducted a meta-analysis of existing competencies in the healthcare system "in order to work toward a common taxonomy. Although there were core similarities across disciplines, there was a need to add, conflate, and eliminate duplications." A sample tweak that evolved from advanced analysis was "broadening the title of one domain from Medical Knowledge to Knowledge of Practice." This adjustment may not seem to be a big one, but it served to expand the application of the competency beyond just a clinical interpretation to a more inclusive one of healthcare professions across the general practice of healthcare.

The National Academy of Medicine "identified 8 emerging areas in need of competency development: informatics, communications, competency-based participatory research, global health, ethics, genomics, cultural competency, and public health and law. While the list of competencies and training needs is robust, it is without clear prioritization. This remains a critical gap in workforce development" (Sellers et al. 2015, S14).

Even if we can imagine one day when a universal set of competencies is established for healthcare; what happens then? The competency is only as effective as it is exercised and assessed to improve performance, and this is where an accrediting body plays a role. The healthcare discipline is only too familiar with certifications and licensing. But, according to the Institute of Medicine (2003a), "accrediting organizations vary in their approach to the core competencies, ranging from assessing such competencies in their standards, to requiring related curricula and education experiences, to encouraging educational institutions to include the competencies."

While working at the National Association of County and City Health Officials, I had an opportunity to liaise with the Public Health Foundation (PHF). The PHF Council on Linkages Between Academia and Public Health Practice worked to develop a consensus set of skills for the broad practice of public health, as defined by the 10 Essential Public Health Services. In June 2014, a set of Core Competencies were adopted around eight domains, reflecting skill areas within public health, and three tiers, representing career stages for public health professionals (Council on Linkages Between Academia and Public Health Practice 2014).

Associating competencies with job descriptions (Public Health Foundation n.d.) makes the annual task of performance assessment that much easier. When a process has a logical application, it is more likely to be used and that is when the system can begin to gain traction.

Perhaps the connection competencies can contribute to our efforts to shift healthcare resides with simply keeping the conversation alive. For example, Friedman (2018) notes, "If the healthcare industry is going to survive and thrive in the years to come, leaders need to quickly adopt a new set of competencies and personal practices: emotional intelligence systems thinking enhanced conversational skills change management embracing chaos and complexity." As new competencies are recognized and added to the mix, at least they direct our thoughts to the possible. What if chaos is a new norm; how would a healthcare team navigate that? I suppose if you ask any emergency management cohort that survived a natural disaster, pandemic influenza, or Ebola, they could shed some light on what skill sets they accessed to cope. It is likely that the lessons learned would then inform another set of competencies.

It is feasible that the potential of competencies might be realized when applied to the system itself. In 2016, the U.S. Department of Health and Human Services launched the Public Health 3.0 Initiative as a call to action for public health to meet the challenges of the 21st century. It urged "a Chief Health Strategist role that requires high achieving health organizations with the skills and capabilities to drive such collective action" (DeSalvo et al. 2017, p. 4). Since "efficiency" was identified as one of the national quality aims, then bundling the collective competencies of a dedicated healthcare workforce toward organizational goals might hold promise.

Whether competencies are universal or specific, static or an ever-morphing entity as healthcare transforms, tied to individual job descriptions or system wide, the promise is in keeping the conversation alive.

Competency Inspired Initiative: Public Health Accreditation Board

One inspirational example of how competencies can grow into a promising practice that is moving the needle for healthcare reform is public health accreditation: a conversation that has taken place over the last 10 years. The PHF Core Competencies were the precursor to the important work of the Public Health Accreditation Board (PHAB). According to Foster et al. (2018, p. S50), "since this framework was well received and understood by the field, PHAB chose to use that as a starting point for accreditation." While serving on the PHAB Board of Directors as an Organizational Representative (Ex-Officio Member), I witnessed firsthand the belief and dedication of the initiative, and its potential to be a game-changer.

Just to put accreditation's potential into perspective, "as of August 2016 approximately 80% of the U.S. population lived in the jurisdiction of one of the 324 local, state, and tribal health departments that has been accredited or is in the process of becoming accredited by PHAB" (DeSalvo et al. 2017, p. 5). A health system operating at optimal level is bound to have a positive impact on servicing its constituents. This demonstrates a direct link between competencies and advancing the healthcare agenda.

A big component of the accreditation program is workforce development, and this makes sense because it is the healthcare professional, working effectively in interdisciplinary teams, that is going to make a difference. In a report marking the 10-year anniversary of accreditation and its impact on the workforce, Ye et al. associate the experience with "perceptions of increased supervisory support, organizational support, and morale, but it is also linked to overall job satisfaction" (2018, S76). "One year following accreditation, 91% of survey respondents said that accreditation has improved their health department's ability to identify and address gaps in employee training and workforce development" (Meit et al. 2017, p. 27). Competencies can impact workforce development by providing a standard to emulate, and they are an essential contributing factor to our national healthcare conversation. The impact of competencies may not always be obvious, but eventually inroads are realized. The connectedness between the PHF Core Competencies and PHAB accreditation efforts provides just one example, and that was a 10-year journey to date.

Competency Framework for an Academic Program

In the Fall of 2014, I started a new faculty position at a college where a Bachelor of Science degree program in Healthcare Management had just been awarded in January of that year. It was evident that optimization of the program was still underway. As I had worked with competencies in past positions, it made sense to frame the emergent program with competencies as the foundation. Unlike some of our allied healthcare counterpart programs that are guided by their licensing board, healthcare managers do not necessarily have a ready blueprint to follow. The HLA competencies seemed to be the most compatible with the role of healthcare managers, and were broad and general enough to serve as a starting point. We would begin with the competencies: communication, leadership, professionalism, knowledge of the healthcare environment, and business skills, as a backdrop of inquiry to build the curriculum.

The Council for Adult and Experiential Learning (2012, p. 8) notes that a competency framework "sends a message to those outside the institution about what a college degree holder should know and be able to do – acquiring skills and knowledge is important for the content." Given the novelty of our program, it would be appropriate to generate awareness of such a budding resource among our regional healthcare partners in the four-county Treasure Coast region our institution serves. Grounding the program on competencies would also signal program credibility, and a desire to provide only the best graduates to fill workforce demands.

The Better Understanding and Learning Design (BUILD) Survey

With the clear intent to construct a program that would not only foster an optimal learning environment for current and future students, but assure career-readiness, more information was needed.

As I processed how to incorporate healthcare competencies into curriculum design, I wanted to align a national perspective with regional viewpoint and relevancy. I developed the Better Understanding and Learning Design (BUILD) Survey to gain understanding of workforce development issues and expectations by regional healthcare partners. In early October 2014, I created a concise 15-question BUILD Survey. Pilot testing of the survey encompassed representatives from the local chapter of the Treasure Coast Healthcare Executive Network, and members of the institutions' Healthcare Management Advisory Committee. The survey was disseminated on October 31, 2014, as an email inviting participants to complete the survey through a dedicated survey web link embedded within the body of the email.

Eighty-eight surveys were sent, and there were 20 email bounce backs with insufficient or inactive addresses, for a grand total of 72 sends. The survey was deactivated on November 14, 2014, after a two-week run with a total of 25 participants for a response rate of 35%.

The survey revealed that Treasure Coast healthcare managers seek employees who perform at higher levels than one might expect for entry-level healthcare professionals with a Bachelor of Science degree. The communication/relationship management competency ranked high at the "expert" level (38%), followed by professionalism (33%), at the same expert level. The competencies of knowledge of the healthcare environment and business skills were ranked by 33% of respondents at the "competent" level. All five competencies were recorded in the "novice" or "advanced beginner" levels. It is clear that potential employees are seeking these skills in their employees.

Based on survey findings, the reader could postulate that competencies in the areas of communication relationship management and overall professionalism are important to potential employers in the region. Another interesting finding was the top trend most likely to occur in the next five years (2015–2020) was a shortage of entry-level healthcare managers (26%). This projection of course matches the national trends we have already discussed.

BUILD Focus Group

On January 22, 2015, a focus group was held to follow up on some of the key findings from the BUILD Survey. The targeted objective for the focus group was to make recommendations to the institutions' Healthcare Management Advisory Committee based on a discussion and interpretation of the survey findings. The audience was comprised of representative regional healthcare professionals and students. Three questions facilitated the process:

- Are we teaching to a "proficiency" performance level?
- Are we addressing the "requisite" competencies and professional skills?
- Are we optimizing capstone opportunities?

For the focus group, proficiency performance level was defined by our Healthcare Advisory Group as "an employee who sees what is most important in a situation, and acts." A consensus was made that this proficiency reads as someone who is a "self-starter" and has "critical thinking" skills. Adding more group assignments was one recommendation to foster proficiency because a team approach is needed when working in today's healthcare discipline. In group assignments, students need to focus on being accountable to their team for their portion of the project.

One suggestion to gauge proficiency was the best practice of "see one – do one – teach one" where there is no room for doubt on the performer's knowledge of the material. Another recommendation was made to institute a leadership academy, much like many Chambers of Commerce have to groom municipality leaders. As a cohort move through the training, they network with area leaders to practice their newly gained skills. Each graduate of the program then pays forward their knowledge gain by modeling the way.

In examining the competency list that informs our curriculum, the focus group noted the current absence of a dedicated communication class. Their recommendation was to omit the epidemiology class, which is not necessarily as germane to healthcare managers as public health personnel, and replace it with a communications class.

The focus group, especially student members, felt strongly that the current capstone obligation was not adding a meaningful opportunity to exercise healthcare competencies. The participants acknowledged the ever-increasing challenges of onboarding volunteers and interns, and the staffing shortages that prohibit taking on another task, such as mentoring. A key recommendation emerged from the focus group to examine the efficacy of the current 15 credit hour per course service learning requirement, as well as the capstone placement requirement.

BUILD Student Listening Session

The intent of the Student Listening Session was to enable a forum for Healthcare Management students to voice comments about their evolving program. The session was held on January 28, 2014, and I co-facilitated it with a capstone student I was proctoring. A modified Appreciative Inquiry protocol was applied to the session. By inquiring about the best past, present, and future experiences associated with an issue, trends emerge which epitomize the shared values of the students. The three prompt questions were:

- Share with us one great past experience with the program.
- Share with us a current exceptional occasion you had associated with the program.
- Post a media headline about the program's success three years from now.

Students shared value in learning from peers and alumni of the program, and in the past, these real world touchstones had meaning. Currently, students enjoyed classes that were based on case studies or real-world scenarios, and they liked the opportunity to network with healthcare professionals through site visits or as guest speakers. In the future, students would like to see the program's reputation grow throughout the region, as partners become more aware of new graduates entering the market. They want to be associated with an exceptional program, and would come back as alumni to serve as role models to new students. Throughout all three questions, students focused the most on real-world career-related scenarios and networking with successful program alumni and practitioners currently working in the Treasure Coast healthcare sector.

Development of a Healthcare Degree Matrix

Informed by BUILD activity findings, it was evident that a competency scaffold should guide every aspect of the program from program learning outcomes to assessments. In all, six steps were identified to fulfill the ambitious goal of designing a Bachelor of Science degree program inclusive of: (1) selection of healthcare management core competencies, (2) determination of program learning outcome, (3) documentation of course identifiers, (4) determination of course learning outcomes, (5) determination of course performance indicators, and (6) recommendation of course assessment. Steps toward achieving our program framework are highlighted below.

Step 1: Selection of Healthcare Management Competencies

In order to determine if the HLA set of competencies were indeed the best possible set of competencies to frame the program around, a number of assets were accessed. A meta-analysis of healthcare competency literature was secured, and our Healthcare Advisory Committee, a group of healthcare professionals who serve a consultative role and touchstone for program relevancy, weighed in. Top-tier skills necessary for a healthcare manager's career success were identified as communication, leadership, professionalism, knowledge of the healthcare environment, and business skills. In essence, we adopted the five competencies detailed by the Healthcare Leadership Alliance (Stefl 2008). Once the basic competencies were acknowledged, subsequent steps could proceed, based on the competency parameters.

Step 2: Determination of Program Learning Outcomes

Considering analysis from step one, it was determined that the five competencies, derived from the ACHE Healthcare Executive Competencies Tool (2018), by the Healthcare Leadership Alliance and the American College of Healthcare Executives, were incorporated into all program syllabi as the overarching program learning outcomes:

- *Communication and Relationship Management*: The ability to communicate clearly and concisely with internal and external customers, to establish and maintain relationships, and to facilitate constructive interactions with individuals and groups.
- *Leadership*: The ability to inspire individual and organizational excellence, to create and maintain a shared vision, and to successfully manage change to attain the organizations strategic ends and successful performance.
- *Professionalism*: The ability to align personal and organizational conduct with ethical and professional standards that include a responsibility to the patient and community, a service orientation, and a commitment to lifelong learning and improvement.
- *Knowledge of the Healthcare Environment*: The demonstrated understanding of the healthcare system and the environment in which the healthcare managers and providers function.
- *Business Skills and Knowledge*: The ability to apply business principles, including systems thinking, to the healthcare environment; basic business principles include (a) financial management, (b) human resource management, (c) organizational dynamics and governance, (d) strategic planning and marketing,

(e) information management, (f) risk management, and (g) quality improvement.

Step 3: Documentation of Course Identifiers

With competencies selected and a program learning outcome identified, step 3 focused on a review of courses against the five competencies. Course identifiers, pre and co-requisites, and sequential placement of courses along a guided pathway, were analyzed.

Step 4: Determination of Course Learning Outcomes

With courses identified and sequences established, the focus of step 4 was assessing how each Course Learning Outcome (CLO) addressed professional core competences. This process revealed strengths and weaknesses of existing CLOs, and allowed opportunity to modify course descriptions as necessary. As we progressed through CLO analysis, our Healthcare Advisory Committee were able to counsel us on the proposed elimination of a Health Information Systems (HIS) course, which focused on coding. Knowledge gained from the HIS course would not be as beneficial to our students, as this skill is generally outsourced by agencies. Given the obvious presence of communication across the literature review of competencies and lack of such a class in our curriculum, a new communications class was an apparent replacement for the deleted HIS course.

Step 5: Development of Course Key Performance Indicators

With solid CLOs, step 5 focused on development of Key Performance Indicators (KPIs) for each course. Each KPI was evaluated for translation to reflect the student's ability to perform the role of a healthcare manager.

Step 6: Recommendation of Course Assessment Methods

Step 6 called for a meta-analysis of assessment methods. Course assessment needs to be a flexible process in consideration of the variety of student learning modalities such as visual, auditory, and kinesthetic. Assessment also considers the desired end point of learning: knowledge, reasoning, performance, and/or ability to create a product. Each end point can then be evaluated through a respective method: criterion, diagnostic, formative, and summative. Given the complexity of contributing elements, a variety of assessments should be attributed to each course. To simplify the maze of assessments, we started with a basic assumption: does the assessment assure our students are career-ready?

The abbreviated overview of competencies provided in this chapter is designed to nudge a thought process on the linkages between grooming a healthcare workforce, in as much transition as the healthcare system, and imagining potential in such a vision. Academia plays a pivotal role in nurturing this connection. One novel Bachelor of Science in Healthcare Management program positioned a competency groundwork for the curriculum. In the next chapter you can read what ascended from that foundation.

References

ACHE Healthcare Executive Competencies Assessment Tool. 2018. "Healthcare Leadership Alliance and the American College of Healthcare Executives." Accessed January 8, 2018. https://www.ache.org/pdf/nonsecure/careers/competencies_booklet.pdf

American Hospital Association. 2017. *Bridging Worlds: The Future Role of the Healthcare Strategist*, 2nd Edition. Accessed July 28, 2018. https://www.aha.org/guidesreports/2018- 06-04-bridging-worlds-future-role-healthcare-strategist

Council for Adult Experiential Learning. 2012. "Competency-Based Degree Programs in the U.S.: 1–52." Accessed

July 30, 2018. http://cdn2.hubspot.net/hubfs/617695/
CAEL_Reports/2012_CompetencyBasedPrograms
pdf?submissionGuid=2709b6a2-7073-4174-a2e7-355bcfa261d

Council on Linkages Between Academia and Public Health Practice. 2014. *Core Competencies for Public Health Professionals.* Washington, DC. Accessed http://www.phf.org/resourcestools/ Documents/Core_Competencies_for_Public_Health_ Professionals_2014June.pdf

DeSalvo, Karen, Wang, Y. Claire, Harris, Andrea, Auerbach, John, Koo, Denise, and O'Carroll, Patrick. 2017. "Public Health 3.0: A Call to Action for Public Health to Meet the Challenges of the 21st Century." Accessed July 30, 2018. https://www.cdc.gov/pcd/ issues/2017/17_0017.htm

Englander, Robert, Cameron, Tereri, Ballard, Adrian, dodge, Jessica, Bull, Janet, and Aschenberger, Carol. 2013. "Toward a Common Taxonomy of Competency Domains for the Health Professions and Competencies for Physicians." *Academic Medicine*, 88(8): 1088–1094.

Foster, Allison, King, Laura, and Bender, Kaye. 2018. "Are Public Health Academia, Professional Certification, and Public Health on the Same Page." *Journal of Public Health Management,* 24(3 Supp): S47–S50.

Friedman, Leonard. 2018. "Transformational Healthcare Leadership Competencies." Association for Talent Development. Accessed July 28, 2018. https://www.td.org/insights/ transformational-healthcare-leadership-competencies

Healthcare News. 2018. "Future for Healthcare Jobs: Seven Charts Show Intensifying Demand for Services and Workforce." Accessed July 28, 2018. https://www.amnhealthcare.com/ latest-healthcare-news/future-for-healthcare-jobs/

Institute of Medicine. 1999. *To Err Is Human: Building a Safer Health System.* Washington, DC: National Academies Press.

Institute of Medicine. 2001. *Crossing the Quality Chasm: A New Health System for the 21st Century.* Washington, DC: National Academies Press.

Institute of Medicine. 2003a. "Chapter 5, Health Professions Oversight Processes: What They Do and Do Not Do, and What They Could Do." In *Health Professions Education: A Bridge to Quality.* Washington, DC: National Academies Press.

Institute of Medicine. 2003b. *Health Professions Education: A Bridge to Quality.* Washington, DC: National Academies Press.

Lipstein, Steven, Kellermann, Arthur, Berkowitz, Bobbie, Phillips, Robert, Skylar, David, Stelle, Glenn, and Thibault, George. 2016. *Workforce for 21st Century Health and Health Care in Vital Directions for Health and Health Care: Priorities from a National Academy of Medicine 1–10.* Washington, DC: National Academies Press.

Love, Dianne, and Ayadi, M. Femi 2015. "Redefining the Core Competencies of Future Healthcare Executives Under Healthcare Reform." *Administrative Issues Journal: Connecting Education, Practice, and Research* 5(2): 3–16.

Meit, Michael, Siegfried, Alexia, Heffernan, Megan, Kennedy, Mallory, and Nadel, Tori. 2017. *Final Report: Evaluation of Short-Term Outcomes from Public Health Accreditation.* NORC at the University of Chicago, 1–71. Accessed August 4, 2018. http://www.norc.org/PDFs/RWJF/NORC_RWJF%20 Evaluation%20of%20Outcomes%20from%20Accreditation.pdf

Public Health Foundation. n.d. "Competency-Based Job Descriptions." Accessed http://www.phf.org/resourcestools/ Pages/Competency_Based_Job_Descriptions.aspx

Sellers, Katie, Leider, Jonathon, Harper, Elizabeth, Castrucci, Brian, Nharthapudi, Kiran, Liss-Levinson, Rivka, Jarris, Paul, and Hunter, Edward. 2015. "The Public Health Workforce Interest and Needs Survey: The First National Survey of State Health Agency Employees." *Journal of Public Health Management,* 21(6 Supp): S12–S27.

Stefl, Mary. 2008. "Common Competencies for All Healthcare Managers: The Healthcare Leadership Alliance Model." *Journal of Healthcare Management:* 53(6): 360–373.

Thompson, Derek. 2018. "Healthcare Just Became the U.S.'s Largest Employer." *The Atlantic.* Accessed July 28, 2018. https://www.theatlantic.com/business/archive/2018/01/ health-care-america-jobs/550079/

Ye, Jiali, Verma, Pooja, Leep, Carolyn, and Kronstadt, Jessica. 2018. "Public Health Employees' Perception of Workplace Environment and Job Satisfaction: The Role of Local Health Departments' Engagement in Accreditation." *Journal of Public Health Management,* 24(3 Supp): S72–S79.

Chapter 2

Professional Development Portfolios

Career Advancement through Professional Development Documentation

There is no doubt that the past couple of decades have been focused on healthcare reform. In Chapter 1, our awareness was elevated about the role the healthcare workforce plays in transitioning to the healthcare system U.S. citizen's mandate. The healthcare workforce is more attuned to the importance of a competency standard, and being held accountable to a mark. Connections between the potential that competency-based job descriptions, performance, and career advancement contribute toward an improved healthcare system should by now be apparent.

In its report *Redesigning Continuing Education in the Health Professions*, the Institute of Medicine states "in theory, the purpose of continuing education is to update and reinforce knowledge which should ultimately result in better patient care." Career Professional Development (CPD), however, needs to go beyond continuing education, and "be an ongoing process that occurs at the point of care, in conversations with colleagues, and in many other ways that clinicians resolve daily problems of patient care" (Institute of Medicine 2010). Findings from the report suggest that for maximum effect, professional development needs to move beyond an individual experience toward a team-based phenomenon.

Examples of CPD practices might include a "structured process for self-reflection, utilizing tools such as a learning portfolio that document practice-based learning/ improvement activities, and address learning objectives/general competencies for inter-professional practice" (Health Services and Resources Administration n.d, p. 18). A group of hospital pharmacists maintained portfolios on competency-based performance, and admittedly the learning curve was steep. However, "the portfolios have helped to identify competency gaps in its staff and spurred the department on to bridge these gaps" (Koh et al. 2017, p. 6). This is an example of how individual effort subsidizes the greater team effort for improvements within a respective discipline.

Portfolios can also be used as a component of an employee's annual review, or for promotion consideration. Chamblee et al. (2015, p. 114) reported portfolio implementation among a group of advanced practice professionals, and detailed the portfolio as "a visual representation of the individual and his or her experience, strength, abilities, and skills. Based on these definitions, an individual's portfolio is a unique professional biography including personal growth and development." In this case the career advancement was based on individual merit, but had a synergistic effect with the team and system, as everyone stepped up their performance.

Service learning has also been applied as an extension of the classroom for a number of academic programs, as a component of a student's professional development. The School of Health Sciences at the National University of Ireland, Galway, examined the impact of service learning for its students, academics, and community. Many students reported that "they were challenged to explain their professional role and knowledge to the audiences…they were forced to reflect on their professional knowledge base and to find new ways of explaining themselves" (McMenamin et al. 2010, p. 502). The experience also served to "break down the traditional barriers that might exist between town and gown." Likely key benefits of the exercise for all parties were demystifying core mission, and raising awareness that theory-based and academic skills will eventually have to be applied when students fulfill career roles.

Typical of service learning, students are positioned within healthcare systems or community-based organizations (CBOs) for intermittent or extended placements. According to Rooks and Rael (2013, p. 95), service learning "bridges classroom learning and community volunteerism and is anchored in the curriculum" but it comes with its own drawbacks. While requiring a service learning component for their social determinant of health courses, students had setbacks with "site selection, site interaction, or meeting the CBOs project goals… students' paid work was the biggest challenge for their service learning experiences."

Rather than discount service learning as a professional development model, we might continue to capture the community outreach aspect, but with more controls for the variables, such as a student's work schedule. There is merit in the dual advantage for students to gain real world exposure, and for CBOs to gain appreciation of their local academic resource as a potential partner for workforce development.

Regardless if professional development is drawn from continuing education, competency-based education, experiential or service learning, the time has come where it must occur within an inter-professional framework to emulate the national movement toward a team-based healthcare workforce. Klein-Collins (2013, p. 7) sums it up best when she states: "in the 21st century book smarts are not enough. The central concept behind competency-based education programs – that it is more important to focus on what students know and can do than how they learned it or how long they took to learn it – also resonates with the public."

Toward a Meaningful Academic Professional Development Process

As our academic program was evolving based on a firm grounding in the healthcare competencies; it seemed the right time to explore professional development options for our students as well. Activities associated with the BUILD initiative definitely informed next steps in designing a meaningful academic professional development process. Based on key findings, the protocol would have to be competency focused, have a data collection and analysis feature, and link to career preparation. Preserving some elements of service learning also made sense, such as contact with the healthcare community as avenues for students to explore and apply classroom learning in a more active manner. Exposing our student profile to potential employers was also a worthwhile component.

Professional Development Service Learning Portfolio

A number of academic programs recommend that students perform service learning within the institution or the community, and this is a good practice, but perhaps it is not enough. Initially, our program, for example, required students to complete 15 hours of service learning for every course credit hour enrollment. A typical student with four classes, or on average 12 credit hours, would be required to complete 60 volunteer hours each semester. Our student profile is comprised mainly of professionals already working in the healthcare field, enrolled as full-time students, and with families or other commitments. In the majority of cases, service learning to our students represented a burden, rather than a component of lifelong learning.

Adding to a sense of disconnect between service learning and potential value added was the fact that students were finding it increasingly more difficult to secure a service learning venue. Potential placements throughout the region were limited for a number of reasons. The practice of onboarding employees also included volunteers and interns, and vetting students who would be on site for a limited number of hours each semester did not have high priority. If a student secured a potential healthcare enterprise to work within, the activities were often limited to tasks such as answering the phone or preparing bulk mailings. It was becoming increasingly clear that service learning alone would not hit the target of a professional development co-curricular activity.

Around the same time as service learning limitations were becoming evident, curriculum analysis of the fairly new Bachelor's in Healthcare Management degree program was underway. Curriculum revisions called for competencies to be embedded throughout courses, learning outcomes, and assessments. The curriculum matrix aligned around five key competencies: communication, leadership, professionalism, knowledge of the healthcare environment, and business skills. Applying the same five competencies as a co-curricular activity would reach beyond traditional classroom learning and contribute to enriching students' advancement toward career-readiness. By combining best practices of service learning and professional development, we arrived at an initiative called Professional Development Service Learning (PDSL).

Beginning in the Fall semester of 2016, the PDSL activity compelling students to explore various opportunities where they could gain experiences in all five competencies was piloted. Students could apply episodes from their current job, a role in the community, or within the institution. The set parameter was that the event had to center on one of the five competencies, and detail how knowledge gained might relate to a future healthcare career. Cultivating a sense of application was a key component because it linked current experiences with future accountabilities.

Working with an existing institutional platform, students were instructed to create their PDSL E-Portfolio by completing an online form. The form had drop down boxes listing each competency and a write-in box for students to record events and outcomes. Ongoing feedback from students indicated that accessing the form was challenging, as a total of five clicks were required to even reach the site. This information was taken into account for subsequent form development because we wanted to encourage the process, not make it difficult. A simplified Survey Monkey™ form was developed, and the URL link was directly available through course shells in the learning management system. Students could access the PDSL Survey with just one click, and submission rates escalated.

The program director compiled survey results into a PDSL report at the end of each semester. Examples of the best experiences and a variety of applications within each competency were selected for inclusion in the report. Names of students were kept anonymous and any indicator of specific healthcare agencies were sanitized. A report was published at the beginning of the subsequent semester and made readily available to students through their course learning management system, which was Blackboard.

The intent of the report was to raise awareness about the competencies, and for students to learn how their peers interpreted each competency. For example, if a student was unsure of what business skills a healthcare manager required for job success, they could focus on the business skills section of the report for insight. Students were encouraged to keep the PDSL conversation alive with classmates, and to recognize the accomplishments of their peers.

As the PDSL portfolio co-curricular activity gained momentum, faculty received reports that students brought their portfolios to interviews, with great success. Students were able to provide samples of course work such as a business plan, which meshed both a course assignment and a business skills competency PDSL submission. The synergy of connections between courses and striving toward career-readiness was catching on.

Professional Development Service Learning Reports

At the end of the Fall 2016 semester, the first summative report was generated from the PDSL portal. From a fluctuating program student population of approximately 260–293, 243 distinct responses from students were gathered. During this pilot phase the response numbers were good, but not 100%. As shown in Table 2.1 PDSL Reports: 2016/2017 Academic Year, a fairly balanced percentage of responses were logged in each domain. During the Spring 2017 semester, students were a bit more familiar with the PDSL portal, which was further streamlined to ease documentation and data retrieval. At the end of the Spring semester, a summative report was generated from the PDSL portal noting 214 distinct responses. There was yet again an even percentage of responses from students.

Reflecting on the first academic year of PDSL co-curricular activities, it seemed that an evenhanded spread of responses was occurring across competencies, as students pursued learning opportunities and documented results in each of the

Table 2.1   PDSL Reports: 2016/2017 Academic Year

Competencies	Fall 2016 (%)	Spring 2017 (%)
Communication	16	24
Leadership	23	20
Professionalism	18	16
Healthcare Environment	24	20
Business Skills	24	20

five competencies. For the second academic year of reporting, however, a more granular analysis was required of students, intended to raise awareness regarding the array of skills that would be necessary as a health professional. The PDSL survey was reformatted to include in the drop down menu a total of 23 sub-competencies under the five competency domains. The sub-competencies were drawn from the American College of Healthcare Executives (ACHE) Self-Assessment Tool, which originated with the work of the Healthcare Leadership Alliance.

A total of 338 submissions were tallied for Fall semester 2017, a nice increase from the previous semester. Spring semester 2018 was the most productive to date with a total of 789 submissions. The boost in spring PDSLs tendered resulted from extra-curricular activities associated with the program's directors award of the Basil L. King Endowed Teaching Chair in the Health Sciences, and associated World Café events, which will be detailed in Chapter 3. As shown in Table 2.2, PDSL Reports: 2017/2018 Academic Year, there are some interesting observations when Fall 2017 and Spring 2018 are analyzed juxtaposed.

Relationship management (48%) was a high-ranking sub-competency in the communication competency in Fall 2017, and students identified skills in listening, teamwork, and emotional intelligence as lessons learned. One student, for example, participated for the first time in a weekly staff huddle to prepare for the workweek. Being new to the team, she was struck by how such a short session yielded such insight into what each member of the floor was responsible for, and how connected they all were to seamless service. She committed to using this activity one day when she is a manager.

In Spring 2018, general communications skills (60%) was the highest ranking subset. The shift in emphasis from the previous semester might be attributed to introduction of a new communications course into the curriculum.

Table 2.2   PDSL Reports: 2017/2018 Academic Year

	Fall 2017 (%)	*Spring 2018 (%)*
Communication		
Relationship Management	48	48
Communication Skills	38	60
Facilitation and Negotiation	14	14
Leadership		
Leadership	44	30
Organizational Climate and Culture	10	11
Communicating Vision	27	16
Managing Change	19	43
Professionalism		
Personal/Professional Accountability	37	26
Professional Development and Lifelong Learning	42	26
Contributions Community/Profession	21	48
Healthcare Environment		
Healthcare Systems and Organizations	14	14
Healthcare Personnel	13	51
The Patient's Perspective	51	16
The Community and the Environment	22	19
Business Skills		
General Management	14	18
Financial Management	10	15
Human Resource Management	7	14
Organizational Dynamics/Governance	7	6
Strategic Planning and Marketing	6	11
Information Management	11	11
Risk Management	19	10
Quality Improvement	26	15

The bounce could also be credited to the World Café co-curricular activities that were unfolding that semester, with an emphasis on conversations with healthcare professionals from the region.

One interesting observation in Spring 2018 can be seen in managing change (43%) under the leadership competency, and healthcare personnel (51%) under the healthcare environment competency, each ranked highest in their respective categories. One could postulate that these numbers were elevated because two institutions in our region were in the midst of merger discussions, which meant that coverage of acquisitions and staffing were often being reported by local media outlets. A number of our students were also currently employed at these organizations and pending changes were of course being deliberated openly by employers. Perhaps it was just a case of heightened awareness surrounding these competencies, but students did embrace the experience as a learning opportunity, and recorded lessons learned.

In Fall 2017, patient perspective (51%) under the healthcare environment was the largest sub-competency. A number of students reported a conscious practice to consider their workplace through the filter of a patient, and not simply as an employee. Elevated cognizance led to adjustments in how students greet patients and their families, and caused them to slow the process down a bit more, for quality interface. Process changes were also implemented in how prescriptions were handed to patients, with a little more care in making sure the patient knew where to fill the script and how to reach out when refills were necessary. Some participants recalled feeling more compelled to answer questions or provide educational materials. Many students documented feeling good about their career choice because they saw a direct correlation between the patient satisfaction and how they fulfill their role.

In Fall 2017, lifelong learning (42%) was a high ranking subset of the professionalism competency. Students reported that in order to fulfill their PDSL requirement, they were more aware of opportunities to grow: on the job, in their communities, and with their peers. Although anecdotal, faculty observed a zest for learning, not only in the traditional classroom setting, but beyond. Instilling this enthusiasm for learning is essential to advancing the healthcare discipline because the field is in transition and change is inevitable.

As interesting as interpretation of student submissions and variances between the Fall and Spring semesters might be, they are simply subjective. The PDSL co-curricular activity was intended to foster career-readiness in our students, and was not a scientific-based endeavor. However, faculty surmised that increased PDSL submissions and in-class student conversations represented an evolving student awareness of competencies. Students were realizing a direct link between competency-based course content, co-curricular PDSLs, and future healthcare management roles and responsibilities. The co-curricular PDSL activities encouraged opportunities to seek and assess new skills toward career aspirations. The grand total of PDSL submissions for the 2017/2018 academic year was 1,127, compared to a total of 457 in the inaugural year; an outstanding achievement! Excerpts from selected student PDSL submissions will be analyzed under each competency in Chapters 4 through 8.

Professional Development Service Learning Applications

Information contained in the PDSL Reports supplemented existing curriculum plans by providing examples, talking points, and case studies. It appeared that a shift was slowly occurring, moving students toward a more career-focused outlook. Course assignments, discussion questions, group projects, and in class participation all included reference to PDSL experiences. One student submission captured just how coursework and competency consciousness meshed:

> *I was at the hospital working one night and administration called for a meeting about infection control. At the end of the meeting our director asked if there were any comments or questions, and usually everyone just stays quiet. However, through my health management classes I am learning new skills that have taught me how to think outside the box in ways that management would. I raised my hand and explained my experiences with infection control on the floor. My input sparked more conversation between employees and management on how we can improve our infection control throughout all three hospitals. I voiced my opinion, and this meeting was not only informative but also motivational. It motivated me to continue voicing my ideas to spark more discussions that could possibly improve the quality of our facility for the future.*

There was spillover to other aspects of the program. Members of the program's student organization, the Student Healthcare Network, believed they could serve as PDSL Ambassadors to assist fellow students with suggestions to source PDSL-seeking opportunities. This in essence was a mentoring opportunity, where students made themselves available to their peers as PDSL subject matter experts. One enticement to being an ambassador/mentor was the ability to complete the PDSL requirement, and so a firm connection was made between mentoring and accountability.

Similar modeling was occurring in classes. Students who were currently not working in the healthcare field might voice concern in class about where they might secure PDSL experiences. Fellow classmates would jump in and make connections; waitressing calls for communication with the public, retail requires business acumen, and volunteering with a health non-profit organization expands knowledge of the healthcare environment. The students were educating peers with discussions through the lens of how competencies would help them succeed in future healthcare management careers.

Members of our Healthcare Advisory Committee highlighted student profiles through partner agencies. Potential healthcare employers were becoming increasingly aware of the level of our student achievements. Faculty reminded students that reports were being shared with regional healthcare professionals to showcase the breadth and depth of student experiences beyond course preparation. As more PDSL interest was beginning to build, and connections were occurring, students were instructed to save a copy of their PDSL Portfolio and bring it to interviews as examples of their work.

Competencies were embedded throughout the curriculum, and the PDSL Portfolio served as a co-curricular supplement to build synergy and strengthen student success. PDSLs were introduced as a programmatic obligation, and necessary for graduation. Although not linked to a grade per individual course, students were required to document their PDSLs submissions each semester, and the cumulative profile was examined in the final course of each respective degree audit. For example, for the Associate of Science in Health Services degree, students had to provide proof of their PDSL portfolio in the Professional Practice Experience class. In the Bachelor of Science in Healthcare Management degree, students analyzed their PDSL profile in the Capstone courses.

Building a professional development portfolio like the PDSL Portfolio yields value-added benefits.

Professional Development Service Learning Portfolio benefits:

- Actively working on strengthening skills needing improvement.
- Assembling a portfolio of talking points for career interviews.
- Being able to say that you have both book knowledge and practical skills.
- Compiling a robust profile of experiences in each competency domain.
- Exploring new competencies in a safe learning environment, as a student.
- Learning from the PDSL experiences of fellow students.
- Networking while enthusiastically seeking PDSL opportunities.
- Ongoing self-assessment of personal and professional strengths.

Based on the momentum and positive response of the single student PDSL Portfolio initiative, we decided to elevate the conversation. In addition to the informal method that PDSLs had been operating within thus far, we decided to establish a more formal venue for students to discuss collectively where they seek competency experiences and what lessons have been learned. The dialogue would also be two-way between students and regional healthcare professionals. This next iteration of PDSLs will be detailed in Chapter 3: Competency Conversations through World Café.

Professional Development: Personal Career Transitioning

The healthcare system is changing and the healthcare workforce is transitioning right along with it, so employees must be able to keep pace with fluctuating demands. Recent influenza outbreaks provide just one example of how healthcare teams had to learn to don personal protective equipment and preform functions out of triage tents set up in parking lots. The practice of ongoing professional development keeps the connection between competencies and accountability uppermost on one's mind, so that when faced with a natural disaster or Ebola outbreak, one will be able to optimally perform.

Making a case for professional development is the story of how Captain "Sully" Sullenberger successfully landed an airplane on the Hudson River in the middle of extreme engine failure. Albeit a first time event, he was able to draw upon years of experience to be able to react appropriately when needed. The ability to know one's craft at such a level reminds me of how our BUILD focus group defined competency proficiency; an employee who sees what is most important in a situation and acts. Whether a pre-careerist student seeking entry into the field, an early careerist still looking for an ideal position, or a seasoned professional taking pride in a meaningful career, professional development holds promise for navigating whichever path you are on.

Pre-careerists need to spend some self-reflective time exploring aspects of a career that resonates with them. Reviewing job descriptions of a number of active job openings will shed light on the duties and expectations of various roles, and LinkedIn is an excellent resource. Our Student Healthcare Network organization routinely offers workshops on how to establish an active and effective personal LinkedIn account. Evaluating websites of potential employers to ascertain vision, mission, and core values, provides insight into whether or not the institution would be compatible. Then, armed with the profile of an ideal position, examine personal accumulated academic knowledge and co-curricular experiences. If there are gaps, seek opportunities to fill the spaces. Begin to generate a personal brand by highlighting strengths, attributes, and examples of successful projects. This is not a static process because with experience, portfolios grow. This stage is preparation for the transition into an ideal career.

A current healthcare practitioner should also maintain a professional development portfolio to be ready for the next step in their career. Opportunities abound within an organization to participate in workgroups, and learn new technology or skills. If the communication competency presents a personal challenge, then volunteer to preside at the next department meeting in order to push your comfort level until it is at ease. Seeking out a mentor is another key component of professional development at this career stage. Someone who has been with the institution for some time better understands corporate culture and best practices, and will be more than glad to share this knowledge. Partnering with a colleague to serve as a peer reviewer could also have mutually beneficial outcomes because we rarely see ourselves as others do.

Seasoned professionals have learned the benefits of professional development. Just as any tenure-track academic will validate, it is important to preserve artifacts of accomplishments, and involvement in projects and performance. At this career stage, return on investment is its own reward, as lessons learned over a lifetime can be shared and reactivated.

Professional Development: Advancing the Institution

An example of a unique institutional professional development application called Insightful Practice combines elements of both self-reflection and follow up coaching. Fourth year medical students are at a critical juncture with their professional development, and an opportunity to learn on the job makes perfect sense. "Insightful Practice has been defined as professionals demonstrating professional responsibility and accountability by demonstrating their appropriate levels of engagement, insight, and action when presented with credible and independent feedback on individual and/or team performance" (Murphy et al. 2015, p. 2). As everyday activities or unforeseen incidents occurred, documentation would be entered on a web-based tool to detail employee function and impact. Students were then given a chance to review the occurrence with a coach and adjust response options for potentially altered outcomes.

A little bit of insightful practice can be seen in the PDSL Portfolio approach. Posting on a web-based portfolio enabled availability and ease of maintaining the professional development practice. Initial student selection of an experience to post onto their portfolio under a respective competency serves as self-reflection. Student posts were presented in reports and eventually discussed in class, or used in an assignment. Often, comments might suggest a different tactic that could have been applied in the experience, and with this feedback, students were acting as peer coaches.

A human resources department might be able to adapt the Insightful Practice model for professional development. Competencies embedded within job descriptions would provide an excellent starting point to frame ongoing reporting criteria. A common platform like Workday, SharePoint, Office 365, or Google Groups, could be easily accessed by the dyad or team to upload reports. The employee's peer reviewer/coach might be tapped from a different department, which would foster multidisciplinary awareness regarding shared roles toward patient-centered care.

Closing Thoughts

Professional development is an aspect of lifelong learning that is essential for the 21st century healthcare workforce. Generating a professional development portfolio can be an individual, department, or institutional endeavor. Identifying specific competencies linked to the organizational mission, or individual job descriptions, provides context for the professional development process. There has to be a sensible reason to sustain professional development activities. Annual performance reviews hold just as much merit as documenting success stories for an annual report. Make your professional development portfolio a yearly accounting of your story. The peer-review aspect of professional development holds promise for expanding a conversation about competencies, which in turn raise awareness and foster a shared experience. The latter is a bonus for multidisciplinary teams, and supports one of the national aims, thus advancing the workforce in transition.

References

Chamblee, Tracy, Dale, Juanita, Drews, Barbie, Spahis, Joanna, and Hardin, Teri. 2015. "Implementation of a Professional Portfolio: A Tool to Demonstrate Professional Development for Advanced Practice." *Journal of Pediatric Health Care*, 29(1): 113–117.

Health Services and Resources Administration, n.d. *Continuing Education, Professional Development, and Lifelong Learning for the 21st Century Health Care Workforce, 11th Annual Report to the Secretary of Health and Human Services and the U.S. Congress.* Accessed August 11, 2018. https://www.hrsa.gov/advisorycommittees/bhpradvisory/acicbl/Reports/eleventhreport.pdfolmboe

Institute of Medicine. Committee on Planning a Continuing Health Professional Education Institute. 2010. *Redesigning Continuing Education in the Health Professions.* Washington, DC: National Academies of Medicine. Accessed August 11, 2018. https://www.ncbi.nih.gov/books/NBK219809/

Klein-Collins, Rebecca. 2013. *Sharpening our Focus on Learning: The Rise of Competency-Based Approaches to Degree Completion.* 1–22. National Institute for Learning Outcomes Assessment. Accessed August 11, 2018. http://learningoutcomesassessment.org/documents/Occasional%20Paper%2020.pdf

Koh, Sei, Wong, Camilla, Yee, Mei, Samarasekera, Dujeepa, and Lim, Mun. 2017. "The Use of Portfolio to Support Competency-based Professional Development of Pharmacists in a Singapore Tertiary Hospital." Accessed August 18, 2018. https://www.mededpublish.org/manuscripts/1121

McMenamin, Ruth, McGrath, Margaret, and D'Eath, Maureen. 2010. "Impacts of Service Learning on Irish Healthcare Students, Educators, and Communities." *Nursing and Health Sciences*, 12: 499–506.

Murphy, Douglas, Aitchison, Patricia, Santiago, Virginia, Davey, Peter, Mires, Gary, and Nathwani, Dilip. 2015. "Insightful Practice: A Robust Measure of Medical Students' Professional Response to Feedback on Their Performance." *BMC Medical Education*, 15(125): 1–11.

Rooks, Ronica, and Rael, Christine. 2013. "Enhancing Curriculum through Service Learning in the Social Determinants of Health Course." *Journal of the Scholarship of Teaching and Learning*, 13(2): 84–100.

Chapter 3

World Café

World Café Overview

In a previous chapter, I detailed the process of bringing our academic program curriculum into alignment with a grounding in healthcare competencies. The co-curricular PDSL portfolios were also examined as an opportunity for students to further explore the transitional nature of competencies and document lessons learned. In August of 2017, I was awarded the Basil L. King Endowed Teaching Chair in the Health Sciences. The focus of my endowment was an expansion of the single student PDSL activity into a collective competency conversation. In this chapter, I will explore the World Café as a guided protocol to keep the competency conversation alive, and share the step-by-step process for facilitating both a student, and joint student and healthcare professional World Café session.

"World Café, is a simple yet powerful conversational process for fostering constructive dialogue, accessing collective intelligence, and creating innovative possibilities for action, particularly in groups that are larger than most traditional dialogue approaches are designed to accommodate. The image of a café sets the stage for the informal setting for conversation, much as when friends or colleagues meet over coffee to discuss mutually interesting issues" (Brown and Isaacs 2005, p. 3). Although the concept seems simple, it has the potential to yield insight and advance understanding of issues.

In a World Café, participants move from table to table and interact with varied guests around a different topic, or aspect of a larger topic. In this manner, the evolving rounds of conversation are individually focused, but still part of the larger conversation. Once table rounds have been completed, the findings from the collective conversations are debriefed, and the cohort validate their collective voice regarding the content. This endorsement fosters strong ownership of both the content and intent to apply fresh insights.

There are seven principles at the core of World Café, and after 23 years of proven efficacy, it is important to honor the tried and true philosophy.

Seven World Café Principles

- Defining Purpose and Context
- Creating a Hospitable Space
- Posing Questions That Matter
- Encouraging Everyone's Contribution
- Connecting Diverse Perspectives
- Listening for Insight
- Sharing Collective Discoveries

Principle 1: Clarify the Purpose and Set the Context

The decision to host a World Café should be guided by the relevance of the issue, and whether or not it has been adequately addressed by parties affected by the outcome. Bringing students, employees, or clients together in a World Café experience for the purpose of discussing healthcare competencies makes sense. Competencies can be broad, complex, and open to individual interpretation, and so the more perspective you can foster on the issue, the better.

An academic program might facilitate a World Café to simply build awareness about competencies. The reason a healthcare organization manager might bring staff together is to brainstorm projects associated with each competency. The context in both instances is to generate as many ideas as possible, and to explore and expand thinking on the issue, and not to solve a problem.

Once context is clarified, the decision of potential participants can be made. The World Café organizer, who is likely also the host, has to decide who has a vested interest in the issue, and can contribute a unique viewpoint. In an academic environment, including both lower and upper grade level students has the potential to yield an array of experiences. Students who have a few examples to share on how they exercised a competency and the lesson learned will both encourage and inform the student who is new to competency professional development. In the context of an employer seeking input, it might appear that personnel who know the organizational culture and have been on the job for some time may be better suited to participate. Although it is true that seasoned employees have institutional history about what has been tried in the past, and could contribute this insight to the conversation, new personnel bring a fresh perspective to the table.

Deciding upon the context and participants will lay the groundwork for a successful World Café and cannot be taken lightly. One way to initiate this effort and gauge interest is through informal topical conversations prior to even scheduling a World Café. A marketing manager unable to discern the best approach to incorporating social media into the organization might begin to pose a specific query at departmental meetings, and assess responses. Gauge who seems interested in the issue, and what is their knowledge of the topic. After repeating this line of inquiry for a while, the likely subjects, purpose, context, and participants, will emerge. In our academic setting, the buzz around competencies and application of the PDSL portfolio for documenting interpretation of competencies, was genuine. It was the right time to open the conversation up to the whole, and broaden both knowledge and understanding of the growing momentum.

Principle 2: Create a Hospitable Space

When planning a World Café, it is important to consider how the setting will contribute to creating a welcoming atmosphere. The ambiance that Brown and Isaac (2005) originally established was the quintessential small European bistro with red-checkered tablecloths and a candle stuck in a wine bottle dripping wax. This may or may not work given fire codes in respective municipalities, but you get the idea: informal and welcoming.

Consider a location that is open, safe, and inviting. For our project, we opted to leave the traditional classroom setting and selected instead a conference center on campus. The larger room allowed for a professional setting with room for round tables, refreshments, and most important: a different learning environment. Organizations may consider going off-site to a local conference facility, or a venue within the facility used for special events. The environment signals that the experience will be outside the norm and requires a different level of engagement.

The room should have sufficient space to accommodate the opportunity for participants to speak freely and listen without distraction of nearby tables. The perfect environment is only part of the equation for a successful World Café, and inquiry is another key ingredient.

Principle 3: Explore Questions That Matter

Depending on the purpose and context of your World Café, you may explore a single question, or several questions that clarify a larger issue. Deciding on the World Café question is critical to the success of the conversation, and should be well thought out and crafted. Is the question one that has yet to be fully answered by the stakeholders; is it thought-provoking and energizing; will the response open new opportunities? The question should be clearly stated, and not loaded with assumptions.

For our PDSL World Café Conversation, we had an overarching question on how students might facilitate Professional Development Service Learning co-curricular experiences in each of the five competencies. Sub-competency tables each addressed a sole competency. We surmised that through several rounds focusing on each competency, the broader question would be addressed. Please refer to Table 3.1 PDSL World Café Conversation Questions for specifics.

When addressing questions that matter, it is important to support a logical progression of discovery throughout several rounds of dialogue. For example, an organization seeking input

Table 3.1 PDSL World Café Conversation Questions

Overarching Question	
How can Healthcare Management students facilitate Professional Development Service Learning co-curricular experiences in each of the five competencies?	
Sub-Questions	
Question 1	What opportunities have you had to improve your professional communication skills?
Question 2	Where have you experienced opportunity to hone your leadership skills?
Question 3	How have you expanded your professionalism competency?
Question 4	Where have your found opportunity to improve your knowledge of the healthcare environment?
Question 5	What types of business skills have you acquired outside of the classroom?

on an issue may wish to pose the inquiry: how can social media be a component of how we fulfill our communication competency? The inquiry may require table questions on various types of social media – Facebook, patient portals, and Twitter accounts. The conversational rounds could just as easily focus on the definition of the agencies communication values; one table might answer a prompt about transparency, and another about inclusion. Irrespective of how the question or questions are crafted, the key to deep insight is to gain as much perspective as possible, which leads to Principle 4.

Principle 4: Encourage Everyone's Contribution

With purpose and context set, the ideal participants selected, and the best question(s) crafted, the next step is to set an environment that encourages everyone's contribution. Setting ground rules will help this process. For example, the table host has the responsibility to encourage everyone to contribute their ideas and perspectives, and stress that there are no right or wrong opinions, as long as they pertain to the question posed for each respective table.

One way to make sure that everyone's voice will be heard is to paraphrase key points already made by previous table guests, and use them as a springboard to dig deeper into concepts. Listening is an essential skill in this process. The table host models this behavior by paying attention to the speaker and documenting their comments. Using sticky notes, 3×5 cards, or post it notes is one way to record key points as they are shared. Capturing participant comments in one or two words and recording them on chart paper draped over the tablecloth is another option, and encourages table guest to also record their ideas. Monitoring any cross conversation occurring when someone is speaking is another way to keep the table group focused. The table host acknowledges linkages when ideas stated by one guest contribute to insights of another guest.

Principle 5: Connect Diverse Perspectives

A vital component of the World Café is to generate as many ideas as possible and connect the diverse perspectives of all participants. The table host remains at the table to recap ideas already presented and encourage new table guests to actively contribute alternative viewpoints.

As ideas are added to the conversation and associations are made, new discoveries to an ever-widening circle of knowledge emerge. The time intervals to prompt table change may vary based on the number of individuals in a group, the topic, or time constraints. The host will announce when it is time to switch tables, and encourage participants to seek an alternate table with as many new participants as possible.

Principle 6: Listen Together for Insight

At the start of each table switch, the table host facilitates quick introductions, provides a preliminary report of top-tier themes contributed by previous table guests, and requests: please add something new that we have not yet mentioned. These report outs set the stage for new insights into concepts shared by previous table guests, and invites new ideas. It is important to include all ideas, whether popular or controversial, because each new table group has unique insight and experience with the material. What might have been a talking point for one group could be the big "aha" moment for the next. In this stage, listening for insight means keeping the momentum alive and not allowing a lull in conversation.

Principle 7: Share Collective Discoveries: Debriefing the Data

The final principle of World Café is to share all the discoveries related to the question or questions, and to make sense out of the collective voice. Many methods can be applied to data collection and debriefing. Whether the table groups use sticky notes or 3 × 5 cards, all themes are clustered into categories such as top tier, still deciding, or parking lot. Some collections of ideas will be evident, and these are themes that were emergent across all guests that rotated through the topic tables. Ideas recorded on cards or sticky notes labeled as "still deciding" are generally controversial or innovative, and are still peculating among participants. It is important to post such ideas because with insight from the larger group, the concepts may be clarified and moved into another category. The "parking lot ideas" usually turn out to be outliers, and do not fold into the final analysis.

The table hosts post materials on a wall that is accessible to all participants. This method is sometimes referred to as open space or inquiry walls and serves the purpose of displaying all data. It might be helpful to think about the wall as the story written by the participants, who are the actual authors of the posted sticky notes or 3 × 5 cards. A break is recommended at this point in the World Café to allow time to post findings, but also for participants to reflect on the comments. Individuals will look for their comments to be posted, or incorporated into a train of thought. The visual proof of seeing their voice represented, serves to validate ideas of the collective and articulate next steps.

World Café Host Role

With a firm understanding of World Café principles, it becomes clear that the role of a proficient World Café host is essential. The ideal host would be an individual with a vested interest in the outcome of the conversation. An academic program might call on the Dean or Program Director to be the host, an organization may seek support from the Human Resources or Training Director, and communities generally select a key stakeholder in the respective movement.

Depending on the size of the proposed World Café, multiple hosts may be necessary, but it is a good idea to have one individual in the main role.

The host should be well versed in the subject matter and the World Café Process. They should be sincere in the desired outcome to amplify insight into the inquiry. Remember that the purpose for a World Café is to learn more about an issue that has yet to be fully addressed by a smaller group, one that requires the collective voice. Brown and Isaacs (2005) note that being a host requires being fully present, and connecting people at many levels as the meaning unfolds. The host sets the emotional tone for the World Café, and calls participants to recall the last time they had a great conversation; remember what that felt like, and what happened next.

Pre-planning for a World Café will likely be a committee effort, but the host should take responsibility for setting expectations and managing the logistics during the event. I served as the host for our two student-centric and one joint student and healthcare professional PDSL World Café Conversations. As participants entered the venue, I greeted them and invited them to join a table. Once everyone was seated, I provided an overview of the agenda, brief summary of the PDSL project to date, and reminded everyone of Café etiquette. During the event, I roamed around the room to notice how table hosts were managing their group, and to ascertain if any assistance was needed. I prompted table switches at a set time interval, announced break, and facilitated the debrief report outs. There are a lot of components to keep track of, and so it is recommended that a first time host have a trained back up host to trouble shoot any issues that might arise.

World Café Table Host Role

The table host anchors a table, paraphrases comments for subsequent rounds of guests to the table, tallies the collective voice of all that attended their host space, and presents the findings in a fair and balanced way.

Schedule a table host training well ahead of the targeted World Café to allow sufficient time for the table host to practice and feel comfortable with their roles and responsibilities. We were going to host a PDSL World Café in late October, and therefore scheduled a table host training for early September. Our training was initially scheduled for September 9, 2017, but Florida was hit with Hurricane Irma, and we had to cancel. The excitement among students regarding the training opportunity was unmistakable because they were even ready to carry through with the training, despite the institution being shuttered. The natural disaster caused us to re-schedule the training for early October.

Once a date is set, you next have to decide on how many table hosts you require. We intended to have one overarching question for our World Café, which was going to be discussed through five questions; one for each competency, and one per table. Our PDSL World Café was also going to be facilitated twice in order to accommodate the number of students interested in participating. We trained 10 table hosts in order to have five per event. The roles and responsibilities of a World Café table host include:

- Foster introductions at the table, for each new round of table guests.
- Briefly share key insights from prior conversations, so others can link and build on ideas.
- Keep the conversation active and on point.
- Remind guests at the table to jot down connections, ideas, discoveries, and deeper questions as they emerge.
- Remain at the table when others leave and welcome travelers from other tables.
- Reflect on themes and record themes and key ideas on sticky notes or 3 × 5 cards.

Students who participated in the table host training received a copy of the World Café book, a training manual, a $25 gift card, and a certificate of training. Additional tangible benefits to students were enhanced professional development through training on the World Café method, project management in planning, executing and evaluating training sessions, writing reports, public speaking, and networking with potential healthcare employers. The agenda we applied for the two-hour training is available in Table 3.2.

Feedback from students trained as World Café table hosts was encouraging and they felt they had learned a worthwhile skill. The role-playing aspect of the training was most beneficial in building a rapport and a comfort level with the mechanics of both keeping a conversation going and simultaneously recording comments. Students exchanged ideas of how best to accomplish the task.

Comments made on the training evaluation form were encouraging because a key indicator for success in the upcoming PDSL World Café Conversations was how well students understood their role and responsibility as table host. All trainees denoted their readiness to perform. An anecdotal

Table 3.2   PDSL World Café Table Host Training Agenda

Time	Activity	Responsible Party
9:00–9:30 a.m.	Overview of World Café	Trainer
9:30–10:00 a.m.	Role-play table facilitation protocol	Trainer and participants
10:00–10:15 a.m.	Break	Participants
10:15–10:40 a.m.	Role-play debrief protocol	Trainer and participants
10:40–10:50 a.m.	Closing questions and evaluation	Trainer and participants
10:50–11:00 a.m.	Presentation of certificates	Trainer

training evaluation occurred over the next several days post-training, when students enthusiastically promoted the PDSL World Café Conversations to their peers in classes and through social media. This served to bolster interest and registration for upcoming seminars.

Hosting a World Café

We have covered the principles of World Café, the role of the host, and table host responsibilities, and will turn our attention now to the participants, venue, agenda, facilitation steps, and debriefing.

Inviting Participants

Our target for the first two PDSL World Café Conversations was a mix of students who were new to competencies, and those who had successfully had a couple of semesters submitting competency stories to their portfolios. We also had a target in mind of around five to six students for each of the five competency table topics; around 30 students. We felt this number was a good starting point to gain sufficient insight into how students were interpreting competencies.

Faculty announced the upcoming World Café, notices were placed on the course learning management system, and as always, the table hosts continued to be our best word of mouth advertisers. One Quality Improvement class, that normally convenes on the same night as the scheduled event, petitioned their instructor to attend the event.

Venue and Setting

For our PDSL World Café, it was important to host the event in a non-classroom setting to signal that this learning opportunity would be different. We scheduled a large room on campus, generally used for workshops or conferences. The room was set up with five tables, each clearly labeled with a tent card and a different colored theme to distinguish the table topics. For example, the Communication table was green, and all the handouts, props, sticky notes, 3×5 cards, and markers at that table were green. The Leadership table had a blue theme, Professionalism was orange, and so on.

Participants quickly picked up on the setting, which underscored the five distinct competencies. A café theme was accentuated by placement of battery-operated candle centerpieces and flowers at each table. A sheet of flip chart paper was placed diagonally across the colored tablecloths, with a few prompts already written on it, encouraging table guests to write down their thoughts and ideas. Finally, light refreshments were staged at a long table in the room, and students knew by the agenda that they would be made available during the World Café break. Overall, a festive theme was established, and yet there were sufficient cues that work needed to be done.

Establishing a World Café Agenda

We scheduled a two-hour time block to accomplish our PDSL World Café Conversation, and met from 5:30 to 7:30 p.m. Our agenda can be reviewed in Table 3.3 – PDSL World Café Conversation Agenda – and is just one example of the possible flow of a session. The reader will see that we allowed just 15 minutes per table round of conversation. This may seem somewhat limiting, but we had five rounds to complete, and had to allow time for participants to travel to all tables. The evening did not seem at all rushed, however, and the objective of raising awareness and fostering dialogue around the competencies was achieved.

Table 3.3   PDSL World Café Conversation Agenda

Time	Activity	Responsible Party
5:30–5:40 p.m.	Welcome and Overview	Host
5:40–5:55 p.m.	Round 1 Questions	Host and Table Hosts
5:55–6:10 p.m.	Round 2 Questions	Host and Table Hosts
6:10–6:25 p.m.	Round 3 Questions	Host and Table Hosts
6:25–6:40 p.m.	Round 4 Questions	Host and Table Hosts
6:40–6:55 p.m.	Round 5 Questions	Host and Table Hosts
6:55–7:05 p.m.	Break	Participants
7:05–7:25 p.m.	Debrief	Host and Table Hosts
7:25–7:30 p.m.	Closing Comments	Host

World Café Facilitation Steps

Our attendance target was approximately 30 students per session for our PDSL World Café. The following steps were coordinated for a seamless event:

- The room was set up with five round tables, one per competency, with six chairs placed at each; five for students and one for the table host.
- The moderator welcomed participants and provided an overview of the World Café objectives, supported by a PowerPoint presentation.
- Once cued to begin the session, table hosts posed their specific subset question to table guests, and suggested an example or two of possible responses. For example:

    Table host: *Welcome, my name is Krista, and I'd like you to share the opportunities you may have had to improve your professional communication skills? For example, during Fall semester, a student reported being asked to run a staff meeting, and another to facilitate a conflict resolution situation in their department. What other communications experiences have you had…*

Participant: *Well, I had a patient yell at me over the phone just last week.*
Table host: *What did you specifically do in this case?*
Participant: *I listened and then addressed the patient's concerns one at a time.*

∎ Table hosts encouraged ongoing commentary and recorded comments on 3 × 5 cards.

For example, in the exchange demonstrated above, the table host would record a couple words on the 3 × 5 card that captured the idea, listening before taking action.

∎ The host announced when it was time to shift tables.
∎ The table hosts briefly recapped ideas generated from previous table guests, and posed the inquiry for the new table guests.
∎ The table hosts recorded new ideas or expanding on existing commentary.
∎ At an appropriate time interval, the host announced another table shift. This process continued a total of five times so that participants had an opportunity to "travel" to all five competency tables.
∎ The host announced when the conversations were concluded, and invited participants to take a short break for refreshments.
∎ During the break, table hosts arranged 3 × 5 cards under a banner header with their "table question." Ideas with themes were clustered together, some 3 × 5 cards were placed under a "still deciding" section of the banner, and outliners were placed at the bottom of the banner expansions.
∎ When the break concluded, the host convened participants in a semi-circle around the wall where comments were displayed, and encouraged a reflective moment to quietly review the output.
∎ As the host prompted, each table host debriefed their table findings, and invited questions, clarifications, or reductions, from all participants. The process was

repeated until all competency tables had a chance to report out.

■ The host provided a summative statement and thanked participants for their valuable input to the vital conversation.

Steps for facilitation of a World Café session will, of course, vary depending on the nature of the inquiry and the audience. With fewer questions, more time may be allocated to table conversation or the debrief process. These variances are acceptable just as long as the seven principles are honored. It is not a surprise that the World Café community is generous in providing free materials to make a session successful, because after all, the philosophy is to keep the conversation alive and vibrant. I would recommend that anyone contemplating hosting a World Café visit the website at http://www.theworldcafe.com/key-concepts-resources/world-cafe-method/.

A final closing thought about honoring the World Café method seems appropriate for this section on facilitation. In all the times I have hosted a World Café, debrief is the most invigorating. All the hard work of selecting the best venue, crafting the optimal question, inviting the appropriate audience, and training top table hosts, contribute to this yield. There is integral energy in experiencing the amassed voice of the collective, knowing your own voice is represented. The story being debriefed at that very point in time will not be replicated; it is as unique as the authors present and contributing.

World Café Debriefing

Student Conversations

Two Student World Cafés were held with a total of 60 participants. A wealth of insights were realized in the form of one or two word "ideas" recorded on 3 × 5 cards and posted on the open space wall. The findings from these debriefs will be covered in detail in Chapters 4 through 8.

It is interesting to note that as students answered inquiries about where they might seek experiences in each competency, conversations naturally turned to lessons learned from experiences encountered in the respective competency. It was obvious as the sessions went on that one World Café tenant was being artfully practiced by all table hosts: Principle 6 – Listen Together for Insight. The students needed to share their lessons learned more than generate examples of where to look for experiences. Table hosts were taking their cues from the majority of their table guests and allowing the process to unfold.

All input was collected to represent value for those students who shared their stories. Following the two World Café sessions, a summative report was generated and distributed to all students in the Healthcare Management Program. The intent of sharing this data was for students to learn from their peers about how to seek and document experiences in all five of the identified program competencies, and understand take away lessons from each competency.

An evaluation was disseminated at the end of both student-centric World Cafés, and one of the questions gauged interest in keeping the World Café format alive. Students overwhelmingly felt positive about the experience and 97% said they would attend another World Café; they felt the competency conversation was worthwhile. In addition to general feedback on the agenda, venue, and refreshments, a write in area for general comments yielded some affirming thoughts.

Feedback 1

Gaining trust is an important factor in any aspect of life. The World Café discussion allowed me to get closer to my fellow classmates and hear what they

*had to say about their personal experiences. Not
only did they share their experiences with me as the
leader but with the other students that participated
in the discussion. It allowed all of us to interact and
share similar or unique experiences. The atmosphere
was relaxed and comfortable, allowing individuals
to feel comfortable sharing their ideas on the
different topics.*

Feedback 2

*The goal of the discussion for my group was to get
different perspectives when it came to the healthcare
environment. Some students had no interaction yet in
working in a healthcare environment, but shared a
personal experience they may have had when visiting
a healthcare facility. This was a learning opportunity
for all involved.*

Feedback 3

*I think this World Café event was probably one of the
top activities that really put the competencies to the
test and assisted in strengthening my skills. As a table
host, I practiced being able to communicate effectively
and collaborate with each group that visited my table.
I also demonstrated leadership in getting the groups
to start the conversation and keep the focus on the
specific topic. This event gave me an opportunity
to practice the communication and leadership
competencies.*

Feedback 4

*I was the last table host to debrief my table. I was so
nervous, I did not want to do it, but I knew once it
was done I could sit back down with my table group.*

*I made the room laugh when I shared some of the
sayings gathered from my table group when I stated
that – even if you are the CEO, COO, or manager
on shift, your title does not exempt you from rolling
up your sleeves in terms of getting dirty and helping
your coworkers to get the job done. I became more
confident when public speaking after this event and
I am continuing to push forward in silencing my
nerves and getting the topic across the board for
others to hear.*

Student and Healthcare Professional Conversations

Our third and final World Café was a joint session with
students and healthcare professionals.

In this World Café, our healthcare management partners
served as the table host, and we had two hosts per table of ten
students, for a total of 60 participants. The same overarching
question was posed regarding how students facilitate Professional
Development Service Learning co-curricular experiences in
each of the five competencies. The table questions for each of
the five competencies also remained the same. However, based
on our debrief experience from the student-only sessions, we
encouraged tables to also discuss how they interpret, and how
they define, excellence within each competency.

The interchange and findings for this World Café differed
slightly from the student-only sessions because some of the
examples were more specific. For example, a robust discussion
from the Healthcare Environment Competency 3 × 5 card
postings addressed how personnel become more aware of
organizational culture during a merger. As this phenomenon
was currently occurring in our region, both parties have
a vested interest in the outcome. It appeared that students
benefitted from the insights of the healthcare professional
hosts by drilling down to real-world examples of how
competencies will be challenged and managed on the job.

Final evaluations from this joint World Café matched the general sentiments of the first two sessions: positive experience, would participate again, and appreciate being heard. Our healthcare partners were pleasantly surprised to see the level of competency understanding and practice our students were engaged in, and let them know it. The exchange was mutually beneficial to all participants. Our partners noted:

Partner Comment 1

This was a unique opportunity. I gained so much insight into how advanced your students are in their understanding of the healthcare field.

Partner Comment 2

I'd never heard of World Café before, but now that I have experienced it, I am going to see how I can apply it at the hospital.

Partner Comment 3

I am glad that you asked me to participate because I learned from the students just as much as they did from me.

Partner Comment 4

Students were so eager to share, and our table scribe really did a great job in reporting – she captured all the highlights of our table conversation.

PDSL World Café Lessons Learned

Overall, we had 120 participants across three World Café sessions. We initiated the project to foster a conversation around how students facilitate PDSL co-curricular experiences in each of the five competencies. The intended line of inquiry was based on student feedback after the PDSL Portfolio initiative launched, which implied that students were unsure where to seek out experiences that would yield competency insights. Perhaps we failed to check an assumption of how unfamiliar students still were with competencies, a year on, which is when the World Cafés were scheduled.

As sessions unfolded, we had an epiphany; our students seem to already know where to seek competency experiences. The majority of our student body are already working in the healthcare field, and so have the opportunity to seek and apply competency discovery on a routine basis. Only a few of the participants, not currently employed in the healthcare field, were unsure of how to source competency application venues. However, as all students traveled to the various tables and engaged in conversation, the focus shifted to interpretation of each competency.

The real harvest from the World Café initiative was student empowerment. Students served as table host and succinctly debriefed the collective voice of their peers. Moreover, students acknowledged they have applied, or have awareness of how to apply, the competencies demanded of their discipline.

Promising Healthcare-Focused World Café Applications

There are numerous examples of World Café applications in the healthcare field that address the viability of the method. One dual study in Ireland and the United States used World Café to query representatives from marginalized communities on health research topics that resonated with them. Although they varied protocols slightly, event sponsors noted "similarities and differences in facilitation of the World Café across two countries demonstrates that the collaborative approach can be replicated and adapted in different settings" (MacFarlane et al. 2017, p. 283).

The Scottish Health Council applied World Café as a countrywide method to improve participation with constituents. Twenty diverse projects were accomplished through meaningful conversations between healthcare professionals and service end users. World Café conversations had a tremendous range from dementia, self-care, engaging older people, breast cancer, hard to reach rural groups, ethnic communities, and mental illness. A detailed report profiles each of the 20 project objects, recommendations, and impact a year on. A helpful tool kit provides guidelines for hosting similar member or community focused dialogues. One agency noted the project "increased the membership and strengthened the relationships amongst existing members." In the future they plan to "continue to develop ideas that enable our member to participate as equal partners" (Scottish Health Council 2010).

The Agency for Healthcare Research and Quality brought together over 50 stakeholders from federal agencies, clinical and public health organizations, consumer groups, healthcare systems, and academia. Through the World Café process, they were able to "develop a vision for their component of the national strategy to promote primary care and community linkages to improve delivery of preventive secrecies, as well as specific strategies to achieve that vision" (Agency for Healthcare Research and Quality 2014).

Universities too are realizing the benefits of World Café. The Community and Health faculty of the University of the Western Cape, in Cape Town South Africa, apply World Café every semester for their students to build awareness about the inter-professional nature of the discipline. According to Filies et al. (2016, p. 232), World Café is "an example of authentic learning … as students participate in real-world problems … are exposed to interprofessional learning opportunities, they are likely to translate these experiences into practice."

The Doctor of Nursing Practice students at Prairie View A&M University applied a World Café format as an assignment in a leadership course. Dawkins and Solomon (2017, p. 639) noted: "the intent is to expand the opportunities for community contact and involvement through transformational dialogue and the collective intelligence harvested from this method. Guests at each table were peers, community members, and previous patients. The topics selected by the students ranged from education and internships to policy and legislation."

Lehigh University applied the World Café with over 100 employees in order to generate ideas to share with the Board of Trustees on fund investment for the institution's future. The host facilitator noted, "no idea is a silly idea, no idea is a wrong idea, and no idea is a stupid idea. An idea can become a kernel for somebody else to build on. By the time we leave, after an hour, that kernel may have grown into a really functional useable idea" (Alu 2016).

A study in the United Kingdom reached out to healthcare professions through World Café to reveal components of a new undergraduate medical curriculum. A number of insights emerged from the experience and study organizers stated, "the World Café produced relevant information from key stakeholders about participants working with the University" (Garner et al. 2016, p. 4). This study seemed most aligned with our efforts because of the interface of college and healthcare community.

It seems clear that World Café has potential for healthcare organizations and academic healthcare programs to hold meaningful conversations on issues that matter. Competency conversations through World Café are worthwhile and can help in interpretation and application of viable skills the healthcare workforce needs to advance healthcare reform.

References

Agency for Healthcare Research and Quality. 2014. "Appendix D: World Café Sessions." Accessed July 15, 2018. https://innovations.ahrq.gov/linkages/appendixD7/

Alu, Mary. 2016. "World Café: A Few Big Ideas for Lehigh." Accessed July 15, 2018. https://www1.lehigh.edu/news/world-caf%C3%A9-a-few-big-ideas-for-lehigh

Brown, Junaita, and Isaacs, David. 2005. *The World Café: Shaping our Futures through Conversations that Matter.* Berrett-Koehler: San Francisco.

Dawkins, Vivian, and Solomon, Abida. 2017. "Introducing the World Café to Doctor of Nursing Practice Students." *Journal of Nursing Education,* 5(10): 638–639.

Filies, Gerard Charl, Yassin, Zeenat, and Frantz, Jose M. 2016. "Student's Views of Learning About an Interprofessional World Cafe Method." *African Health Professions Journal,* 2(Supp 2): 229–233.

Garner, Jayne, Coulby, Ceridwen, and Anderson, Marina. 2016. "Holding a World Café with Medical Educators." University of Liverpool (Open Access Case study). Accessed July 15, 2018. https://doi.org/10.15694/mep.2016.000018

MacFarlane, Anne, Galvin, Rose, O'Sullivan, Madeleine, MsInerney, Chris, Meagher, Eoghan, Burke, Daniel, and LeMaster, Joseph. 2017. "Participatory Methods for Research Prioritization in Primary Care: An Analysis of the World Café Approach in Ireland and the USA." *Family Practice,* 34(3): 78–284.

Scottish Health Council. 2010. Improving Participation. Accessed July 25, 2018. http://www.scottishhealthcouncil.org/patient_public_participation/participation_toolkit/ world_cafe.aspx#.W3clb-hJiic0

World Café. n.d. Accessed July 25, 2018. http://www.theworldcafe.com/key-concepts-resources/world-cafe-method/

Chapter 4

Healthcare Communication Competency

Communication Competency: Impact on Six Aims for Quality Improvement

Communication appears across a number of competency lists for a reason; it is indispensable in accomplishing the six aims for improvement, vis-à-vis healthcare reform. According to the Agency for Healthcare Reform and Quality (2016), the six aims include safety, effectiveness, patient-centeredness, timeliness, efficiency, and equity. These aims represent some lofty goals. Now more than ever, it is obvious that the healthcare workforce will have to be competent in all aspects of communication in order to be successful in closing the healthcare gap in America today.

Safety is listed as the first national "aim," and this makes sense arising from the 1999 Institute of Medicine *To Err Is Human* report, citing far too many medical errors. Good communication plays a major role in preventing errors, mitigating consequences, and learning from incidents. For example, flu outbreaks in hospitals have been thwarted by consistently communicating about hand sanitizing, thus both preventing and mitigating spread of disease. Likewise, lessons learned both during and following H1N1 pandemic planning, 2009–2010, could not have advanced without optimal communication competence. During this timeframe, and as a component of the health department's emergency support function, tabletop exercises were held to gauge surge capacity. After, action reports were generated, distributed, and talked about in order to make necessary improvement in performance. These events necessitated stellar communication within an emergency operations center, and externally to the general public, through a public information officer. We can clearly see that communication plays a vital role in keeping citizens safe through prevention and mitigation.

Effectiveness is the second "aim" with a focus on providing health services without underuse, misuse, or overuse. Given our current opioid epidemic, it seems apparent that over prescribing is a contributing factor. Efforts to tackle such a pervasive health issue demand a collaborative effort across multiple sectors: practitioners, pharmacists, therapists, and patients. Building the requisite teamwork to surmount this crisis compels excellent communication skills.

Patient-Centeredness is the third "aim" and in order for the patient to feel valued, thoughtful communication will have to consider cultural diversity and empathy. For the patient to be heard, healthcare personnel will have to listen to needs, likes, and dislikes about delivery of service and care. According to Radick (2016, p. 33), "some of the greatest opportunities for improving the patient experience – and, ultimately healthcare outcomes – arise from simple concepts such as increasing patient and family engagement through advisory councils and collecting data in real time at points of care…it is a lasting story people will take with them."

Timeliness is the fourth "aim" and something everyone who has ever waited in the lobby for a set time appointment with their physician can relate to. We have a variety of communication channels to impact on this aim, and whether logging in on an iPad or receiving a text about appointment adjustments, keeping the conversation open is imperative. If a flash mob can be organized at a moment's notice, it does seem feasible that arrangements for an annual checkup could be communicated in a timely manner.

Efficiency is the fifth "aim" directed toward reduction of the cost of healthcare. There is a price to pay for everything from anesthesia to a tube of zinc oxide, and also the time and energy affixed to obtaining and utilizing goods and services from A to Z. Communicating an organizational vision and mission sends a message across the enterprise about how business will be managed. Everyday functions can be handled more efficiently when intent, procedures, and protocols are clearly communicated.

Equity is the sixth and final "aim" and denotes that healthcare should be delivered in a just manner, regardless of status. Access to care should be equal opportunity whether patients live in rural or urban locales. Education should not limit how patients are treated by the system. Attributes such as ethnicity, gender, or age, should not impede healthcare. Communicating in an open and transparent fashion will advance equity. Involving patients in a shared vision, and shared decision making about their healthcare, will increase opportunities for equitable service.

Healthcare workers will need to hone facilitation and negotiation skills to assist in navigating fair and balanced health solutions for clients.

When we link communication skills to the six aims, we cover a wide gamut of proficiencies, and of course mastery of these abilities will take a concerted effort. An excellent place to foster urgency to groom communication skills is at the academic level. Students are eager to learn and build awareness of communication. They can model elements of communication with faculty, co-workers, and colleagues alike, as a component of an assignment or for professional self-development. Our program adopted a co-curricular activity that had affinity with the five core competencies embedded in the curriculum. Students sought experiences beyond the classroom, and recorded their lessons learned. Communication was one of the competencies that students exercised, and excerpts and perceptions from their practice are explored next.

Communication Competency: PDSL Insights

Each semester, students submitted PDSLs, which were aggregated into a report for distribution to the students the subsequent semester. During the first academic year of data tracking, just general information was elicited under each of the five competencies: communication, leadership, professionalism, healthcare environment, or business skills. PDSLs for the 2016/2017 academic year analysis ranked communication second in student submissions. During the second year, students were instructed to dig deeper and select from the sub-competencies within each competency domain. The communication competency has three sub-competencies: relationship management, communication skills, and facilitation and negotiation. For the 2017/2018 academic year, communication ranked first among all five competencies.

Under the communication sub-competencies, general communication skills ranked first with an average of 49%, and relationship management came in second at a close 48%. The sub-competency of facilitation and negotiation was a distant third place at a 14% average of total PDSL submissions. Mining meaning from the data was assisted by the stories students associated with each submission. The low offerings under facilitation and negotiation may coincide with limited opportunity to exercise the skill, but for students who did, there were talking points.

Although it might be interesting to analyze percentages, the effort really does not tell the full narrative of what was occurring through the PDSL initiative. The fact that students were purposefully seeking to broaden competency in order to be better prepared for their chosen career is the real storyline. From a variety of PDSL submissions, excerpts from each sub-competency are shared here in order to substantiate accounts percentages alone may not be capable of.

Relationship Management

The following three excerpts under relationship management demonstrate communication skills in taking initiative, observational analysis, and listening with intent. Students learned that relationships are not static; they are actively two-sided, and one side has to take the initiative in fostering a positive exchange. Through observation and willingness to apply knowledge gained from situational analysis, relationships can be improved. Listening is an essential ingredient of good communication, and we may sometimes forget the role it plays. Listening with intent can only improve outcomes of communication.

Excerpt 1

I noticed that the program coordinator was getting quite a few calls, and yet too many were being missed, and it was adding to office tensions. I developed triage guidelines so that calls could be properly directed to the palliative care or clinical care coordinator based on a few prompt questions. Now calls are transferred to the right person enabling departments to be more productive based on patients' needs, from filling prescriptions to organizing referrals from hospitals or other healthcare facilities. Relationships improved in the office based on this simple communications protocol.

Excerpt 2

From September to November, my primary goal was to observe one of the ten physicians working in the group practice. By walking through workdays as a shadow, I acquired knowledge on how to manage relationships with patients. The patients absolutely loved (the physician) for his compassion and kindness, which gave patients a sense of genuine care. I got an opportunity to learn that building strong relationships with patients is the key to better care.

Excerpt 3

A co-worker and I always went on break together and one day she asked me to let her know exactly when I would be ready. I was side-tracked and really busy with a task, and once completed I just went on my break. Later that day I realized what happened and called to let her know I was sorry. I learned that communication is listening more attentively, and honesty plays a big role. It is important not only to co-workers, but to patients and families as well.

Communication Skills

Under general communication skills, students reported on the role of motivation, taking advantage of learning new communication models, and acting as a liaison. Although there were a number of excellent examples, the following three excerpts are shared here based on a representation of the variety of skill opportunities students pursued.

Excerpt 1

My role at work involves daily interactions with customers, as well as associates. I have to coach my associates on brand standards and selling behaviors. I've also developed skills in customer service interactions and conflicts, making sure to assist the customer with his or her issue thoroughly. This experience has taught

*me to motivate myself to provide the best service to my
associates, as well as the customers.*

Excerpt 2

*At my organization, staff had the opportunity to be
trained on AIDET (Acknowledge, Introduce, Duration,
Explanation, and Thank You). I signed up. This
structured format of communication with all customers,
especially the patients, relieves anxiety and increases
customer satisfaction. I am glad I sought it out.*

Excerpt 3

*One day a patient called very upset about a service she
had received at our office. I noticed that most of the
office staff just pass a call like this along. I asked the
patient to explain the situation, and promised I would
share her story with the appropriate manager, which I
did. I acted as the liaison and saved the patient from
more runaround. A few days later, I called the patient
back, and they were pleased with the response. She said
she would even stay with the same physician as a result.*

Facilitation and Negotiation

Although the facilitation and negotiation sub-competency was
the least active under communication, it was nevertheless a
rich repository of experiences and lessons learned by students.
There was a theme under this section, which drew more
from the affective domain than the cognitive one. Students
addressed feelings of honesty and compassion as being
necessary for successful facilitation. The ability to compromise
was listed as a negotiation tactic.

Excerpt 1

*I had to communicate for my patient who could not talk
at all. I became very acquainted with subtle behaviors*

*and understood what she needed. I had to then
communicate to her caregivers in a tactful manner the
changes that I thought would be better for my patient.
I kept detailed documentation on my patient and
updated the family. This particular patient at times was
in my care alone for weeks. I had the trust of the family
and they respected me also because of my honesty.*

Excerpt 2

*I had to have a conversation with an employee
because a number of co-workers stated this individual
was not pulling their weight. This was a long-standing
employee, who had a number of serious issues occur
in a short time span, and I thought that perhaps that
was at the root of the situation. At first this person was
defensive, but I explained in a compassionate tone
that I was simply concerned. I then asked what might
turn things around, and I listened to their point of
view. As a solution, we set up an appointment with
the employee assistance program. By actively listening
we were able to negotiate a resolution.*

Excerpt 3

*One time a family member was upset with the care his
mother was getting and there was a lot of commotion
in the hallway surrounding the issue. I asked the
individual to step into the manager's office, and asked
him to explain his concerns. I found out the particulars
of the situation and arrived at a compromise. Later I
did fill in my supervisor about the incident and how it
was curbed. She was grateful that it did not escalate,
and the patient received improved attention.*

Selection of the above excerpts from student reports represent
a partial sampling of how students frame communication.
Whether a small daily exchange, or a larger incident, each

is affirming. The experiences are also set apart from theory or ideas discussed inside the classroom, and this models the importance of lifelong learning. Disseminating reports allows students to review what their peers are doing under each competency, and may inspire them to expand their comfort level and try new ways of communication.

Communication Competency: World Café Debrief

Through an endowed teaching chair award, we were able to broaden the scope of the PDSL co-curricular activity to a World Café conversation about competencies. The World Café sessions animated the focus of competency experiences beyond what a bi-annual report could accomplish. Over the course of three World Cafés, two student-centric, and one joint student and healthcare professional, the directive was to broadly inquire about each of the five competencies, rather than examine sub-competencies. Students steered dialogue more toward examples of excellence under each domain, with some comment on where they acquired opportunities to field-test and expand competency.

As shown in Table 4.1 World Café Communication Competency Debrief, three overarching themes emerged: general communication skills, timing and delivery of communication, and not making assumptions/listening. Words recorded on 3 × 5 cards reflect table conversations, and group consensus derived from the cohort debrief. From three separate World Café sessions, the list has been consolidated to eliminate duplicate words, sentiments, or themes, and thus rendered down to one concise summary. The words reflect typical lessons learned by students from communication competency experiences.

During the collective debrief of the first student World Café, one of the lengthier discussions surrounded a technique students referred to as the *sandwich effect*. Students explained this as a way of delivering good news, then bad news, and then good

Table 4.1 World Café Communication Competency Debrief

Communication Skills	Timing and Delivery	Not Making Assumptions/ Listening
• Adapting • Being a mentor/ coach • Clarity – When training new hires • Communication • (two-way street) • Conflict resolution • Give positive feedback • Honesty (get to the point) • Keep calm • Knowledge of subject matter • Non-verbal/body language • Project presentations • Small talk – You never know who you are talking to • Speaking with organization's leadership • Verbal vs. written (verbal is best when possible)	• Bad news (start with...you did your best) • Blunt but sugar-coated • Good listening vs. good communicator • Stop and listen, listening = problem solving • Think first – Then act • Timing, saying the right thing at the right time • When you stop and listen (Aha! moments occur)	• Empathy and compassion • Employee's opinions • Positive attitude • Recognize individuality • Staying engaged • Teaching and training protocols – Trust the process

news, to soften the blow of a difficult conversation. It seemed that many students had been on the receiving end of the "technique," but felt it was both fair and an effective form of communication for corrective action objectives. Student consensus was that the "sandwich" was an appropriate method for a manager to interface with their employees, and many were going to practice it when possible, as they prepare for managerial roles.

It is interesting to note that the actual words "sandwich effect" do not appear directly on any 3 × 5 card rendering, but the sentiment is certainly embedded within the cards that were posted on the open space wall. For instance, timing, saying the right thing at the right time, honesty (get to the point), and bad news (start with…you did your best), are all components of the "sandwich." It was important as the host to allow sufficient time for dialogue because the students were owning the story being presented, and there was a solid translation of the competency to career-readiness.

Another conversation that lingered with the group during debrief was the phrase, *When you stop and listen, aha! moments occur.* This particular debrief occurred specifically with the World Café comprised of students and healthcare professionals. There was an acknowledged sentiment that healthcare workers are far too busy for meaningful communications because they are overworked and rushed. This phenomenon transfers onto patients/clients, but also spills over to co-workers. A few participants shared incidents when they could slow down and really take time during an intake exam or facilitating services for a caregiver or family. The quality exchanges, as they were thought of, yielded more satisfaction for everyone involved. The after effects also lingered, because work functions seemed to be more efficient. The conversation about "purposeful conversation" seemed to have significance for both students and healthcare professionals, and served almost as a re-commitment to pay more attention and "do better."

A final posting that garnered a little more attention from participants than others, was the 3 × 5 card that simply stated *empathy and compassion*. Students could relate, and they pursued a healthcare degree because they wanted to help people; these words are embedded within the discipline. One student shared that communication can be just a smile, which communicates volumes. At a time when a patient is most anxious, that simple gesture can have more impact that any prescription or procedure.

There is no scientific data to corroborate whether or not World Café conversations revealed more about the communication competency for students than their PDSL Portfolio submissions did, but that was never the point. The intent was to provide a forum to foster inquiry and broaden understanding about what communication excellence might look like, and that certainly was activated. When you think about it, the very act of holding "a conversation" improved communication competencies of all involved. For our objective, World Café was a promising practice for students, and next we will examine a few communication initiatives from across the healthcare enterprise.

Communication Competency: Promising Practices

In the ensuing years since crossing the healthcare chasm became our national intent, a number of initiatives have emerged to advance the campaign. Communication remains at the heart of the movement, and the healthcare workforce represent the beating of that heart. A focus on patient centeredness is at the top of the list to move the needle on healthcare reform, and improved communications will help us thread that needle.

REDE Model

One promising communication practice is the REDE Model, which stands for Relationship, Establishment, Development, and Engagement. According to Cleveland Clinic physicians Windover et al. (2014, p. 8), "teaching relationship-centered communication to thousands of seasoned clinicians, we nonetheless recognized that many providers did not intuitively view forming relationships with patients as their role." Based on this reality, a project to improve patient relations was going to have to be "informative and also transformative because it challenges users of the model to explore their own assumptions and beliefs about patients and their role as providers."

The REDE model relies on a number of mnemonics to enable quick recall. For example, SAVE stands for Support, Acknowledgment, Validate, and Emotion. These four steps could "save" an exchange with a patient from being less than productive. Another mnemonic is VIEW, which stands for Vital, Ideas, Expectations, and Worries. If a practitioner can "view" the interchange with a client as not only information gathering, but getting to the root of emotions, then it will be a successful conversation. Other features that encourage use of REDE include a wide array of tools available through an online toolbox, which can be easily accessed and applied in any given situation and setting. The tools are also adaptable and flexible to a variety of settings with patients and clients across the healthcare enterprise.

Hospital Consumer Assessment of Healthcare Providers and Systems

One benchmark of just how effective an institution is in patient relations derives from a survey called the Hospital Consumer Assessment of Healthcare Providers and Systems (HCAPHS). According to the Centers for Medicare and Medicaid Services, the HCAPHS survey contains 18 core questions about critical aspects of a patient's hospital experience. In addition to general environmental questions about hospital cleanliness and quietness, several questions directly relate to communication. Patients are asked to weigh in on what communication was like with the doctor and nurse, how responsive was staff, were medications clearly explained, and was discharge information well-defined.

Reimbursements become linked to both performance on patient experience and quality, and so there is incentive to improve communications across the system. According to the

Centers for Medicaid and Medicare Services (2017), "since July 2007, hospitals subject to the Inpatient Prospective Payment System (IPPS) annual payment update provisions must collect and submit HCAHPS data in order to receive their full IPPS annual payment update. IPPS hospitals that fail to publicly report the required quality measures, which include the HCAHPS survey, may receive an annual payment update that is reduced by 2.0 percentage points."

Colwell (2016) notes that "poor communication during a hospital stay can lead to dissatisfaction among patients, families, and clinicians, but most physicians get little training... inpatient HCAHPS scores improved and outpatient patient satisfaction scores increased an average of 92%" when physicians do get training. With results like this, it may seem apparent that all institutions would run, not walk, to their training department to get the ball rolling on communication training. But, there are some roadblocks.

Another hopeful program, also with a mnemonic, originated from the University of West Virginia. Their program is called BATHE, which stands for Background, Affect, Trouble, Handling, and Empathy/Exit. Caregivers rely on the prompts while communicating with patients, as a reminder of what to cover and how to relate. Patients who were recipients of the method "gave their doctors an average score of 4.77 compared with an average score of 4.0 for patients receiving standard care...one of the obstacles was concern that asking the questions will take too much time...in reality BATHE adds no more than five minutes – it seems to add greater efficiency" (Shute 2018, p. 36).

One hospital with specifically low HCAPHS scores related to nursing communications with patients introduced the "Commit to Sit" initiative. "Sitting instead of standing when talking to patients is perceived as spending more time at the bedside and allows an uninterrupted conversation" (George et al. 2018, p. 83). One challenge to implementing the campaign was a "lack of education about the perceived benefits."

Facing low patient satisfaction scores, the Cleveland Clinic made a concerted effort to address communication and patient relations systemically. They formulated a holistic definition so that all players would be on the same page: "the patient experience was everyone and everything people encountered from the time they decide to go to the clinic until they were discharged" (Merlino and Raman 2013, p. 113). The CEO appointed a Chief Experience Officer, who proposed "all 43,000 employees participate in a half-day exercise...sharing stories about what they do – and what they could do better – to put the patient first."

The output from that system wide inquiry included myriad actions that comprise large and small attempts to put people first. A "best practices" department was established. Employees finally understood how important HCAHPS were, and the patients behind the numbers. Bedside response times were monitored and adjusted as needed. Caregivers were encouraged to huddle more often and exchange pertinent data. Trainings on team work were introduced. Employees who went above and beyond were recognized and honored.

Closing Thoughts

It seems to me that the Cleveland Clinic experience mirrors our PDSL and World Café student co-curricular activities in one important way – it is imperative to just keep talking. Holding a conversation, having inquiry, posing what if's – all can lead to something special.

Two other thoughts concerning the promising communication practices come to mind. One is that if healthcare staff do not realize that there is a communication problem within their organization, then how they can correct it? As redundant as it may sound, we have to communicate about communication. Monitoring systems such as audits, self-assessments, trainings, and huddles have to be in place to constantly check the temperature of how an organization is communicating. The second perception derives from the apparent success of using mnemonics. Adopting a practice that is easy to remember and is embedded into routine workload seems to be a winning formula. The more the healthcare workforce keeps communication uppermost in mind and application, the better probability we have of meeting our national healthcare reform goal.

References

Agency for Healthcare Reform and Quality. 2016. "The Six Domains of Health Care Quality." Accessed September 2, 2018. http://www.ahrq.gov/professionals/quality- patientsafety/talkingquality/create/sixdomains.html

Centers for Medicaid and Medicare Services. 2017. "HCAHPS: Patients' Perspectives of Care Survey." Accessed September 2, 2018. https://www.cms.gov/Medicare/Quality-Initiatives-Patient-Assessment-Instruments/HospitalQualityInits/HospitalHCAHPS.html

Colwell, Janet. 2016. "Taking Communication Skills Seriously." American Hospitalist. Accessed September 2, 2018. https://acphospitalist.org/archives/2016/10/communication-training.htm

George, Sibil, Rahmatinick, Shaida, and Ramos, Jhoanna. 2018. "Commit to Sit to Improve Nurse Communicaton." *Critical Care Nurse* 32(2): 83–85.

Merlino, James and Raman, Ananth. 2013. "Health Care's Service Fanatics: How the Cleveland Clinic Leaped to the Top of Patient-Satisfaction Surveys." *Harvard Business Review.* Accessed September 4, 2018. https://www.thechildren.com/sites/default/files/PDFs/harvard_busines_review.pdf

Radick, Lea. 2016. "Improving the Patient Experience: Every Interaction Matters." *Healthcare Executive* 31(6): 33–37.

Shute, Debra. 2018. "Implement a Communication Tool in 5 Steps." *Healthcare Leaders Magazine* 21(1): 36–38.

Windover, Amy, Boissy, Adrienne, Rice, Thomas, Gilligan, Timothy, Velez, Vincent, and Merlino, James. 2014. "The REDE Model of Healthcare Communication: Optimizing Relationship as a Therapeutic Agent." *Journal of Patient Experience*, 1(1): 8–13.

Chapter 5

Healthcare Leadership Competency

Leadership Competency: Assuming Accountability

The watchword for leaders during this transitional time in healthcare has to be accountability. Meeting the Triple Aim objective of improving the patient experience, increasing health of populations, and reducing cost, will take exceptional leaders with strong skills.

"The Joint Commission has reclassified what it used to call 'core measures' as 'accountability measures'...creating a culture of accountability. Blaming and shaming is the death of thinking about how to improve performance" (Ollier 2018, p. 20). When a new CEO took over the Veterans Affairs Maryland Health Care System, he quickly applied an acronym to address a myriad of challenges facing the institution: "ICARE, Integrity, Commitment, Advocacy, Respect, and Excellence" (Ollier 2018, p. 22). ICARE is a strong countermeasure to any attempt to affix blame and shutter the accountability objective. Values inherent in the initiative also exemplify transparency, systems thinking, and teamwork.

Analysis into the tools that leaders actually apply in the field was conducted through interviews with 26 mid- and upper-level leaders. According to Herd et al. (2016, p. 228), the top four themes emerging from the interviews were "change-leadership, self-development, talent development, and team leadership." Interviewees noted that leaders have to constantly analyze the landscape for trends and how they might impact an organization. Self-development denotes awareness and resiliency. Leaders have to not only be self-aware, but be able to sustain their organizational directive. Team leadership entails delegation and establishing a culture of connection and purpose. This one study touched on a broad set of competencies leaders must possess, and each one will be needed to fulfill the obligations of leadership.

Today's leader also has to be able to share organizational vision and lead teams toward that mission. A teaching hospital in Canada sought to develop a program to foster leadership among staff. According to Stuart and Wilson (2015, p. 4), "leadership practice is evolving from a focus on an individual to one that defines leadership as a process… by defining leadership as a process (not a role), healthcare organizations can develop leadership capacity throughout the enterprise."

In order to honor the "process," the Glenrose Rehabilitation Hospital devised a mentorship program for emerging leaders. Three aspects of the initiative made it successful. The first component was taking the time to match the mentor and mentee. There was "an open call for soliciting mentees and mentors would attract individuals who valued the program's benefits and world align with the need for committed time above their work responsibilities" (Stuart and Wilson 2015, p. 4). The second element was a varied curriculum that allowed for lecture and independent work. The third and final piece was a joint project by the mentor and mentee to further solidify the relationship.

If we use accountability and process as a starting framework for leadership development and execution, then we will have a broad canvas on which to craft a conversation about leadership competency. I especially like the concept of process versus role for leadership because it seems flexible and nimble; just what is needed for the work ahead.

Leadership Competency: PDSL Insights

There are four sub-competencies under the leadership competency: leadership skills and behavior, organizational climate and culture, communicate vision, and managing change. During the 2017/2018 academic year, students were required to submit PDSLs under sub-competencies, and leadership skills and behavior had the most submissions at 37%, followed closely by managing change at 31%. For that same academic year, the leadership competency ranked highest for overall submissions, and in the previous year it was part of a three-way tie for first place alongside healthcare environment and business skills competencies. Students were able to acquire experience under each of the four sub-competencies, and a few examples are shared here.

Leadership Skills

There were a number of interpretations about what constitutes leadership, and the student excerpts below speak to that diversity. The first quote clearly addresses the accountability a leader must possess, and tells a true story of going above and beyond the call of duty. A novice employee quickly learned how powerful listening skills are to a leader, especially in getting to know your team. The final submission shares some insights into the benefits of self-reflection. Leaders must be true to their core, and when confronted with tasks, that true nature will guide them.

Excerpt 1

I am learning that as a leader you have to make yourself available when the need arises. I recently got a call from a coworker because she was having trouble getting a test to calibrate on the analyzer. We were not able to rectify it over the phone, so I decided to go into the lab and help her fix the issue. Looking back on this experience, I could have just as easily let her figure it out by herself. But, I knew it could have had an impact on patient care, and I would not feel good if something went wrong. I know that is what a leader would do.

Excerpt 2

I have been in a leadership role in my organization for just six months, and already tried new skills for me. I have had to delegate to make sure things get done in a timely manner. The biggest thing is to listen to associates and both observe and hear their feedback so that I am more aware of their strengths and weaknesses. I am putting together a stronger team, and it's all about connectivity.

Excerpt 3

As a physical therapist assistant (PTA) I had an opportunity to train students prior to graduation, and I accepted the challenge. What I realized was that I started orientating the students to ideas like integrity, dignity, compassion, and striving to be the best PTA they could be. These values were first, before I ever mentioned actual PT skills. When I reflected back on the sessions, I understood that I was really setting the bar high as a leader, and reinforcing these traits for myself also.

Organizational Climate and Culture

The sub-competency of organizational climate and culture garnered the smallest average of PDSL submissions at just 11%, and perhaps this is because students were not comfortable in seeking experiences at an organization-wide level. For example, one student tied her PDSL posting to awareness of her own culture, linking it to patient satisfaction. A few other students also named language translation support services under organizational culture. Another student sought to align a leadership style with existing institutional norms, and experienced good results. The final submission is a bit of an outlier because it was not a direct healthcare example. However, this posting made it to the semester-end report because the student clearly translated the key components of organizational culture into a career application story.

Excerpt 1

We live in a world that is one big melting pot, full of diversity. With diversity comes language barriers, and in my line of wok I meet numerous people who speak Spanish and Creole. Since Creole is my first language, and not that of my co-workers, I thought that it would be a good idea to implement "Language Line" in our organization. Now, we have instant access to translation services without a hitch. My employees are so relieved that we have this service. They know they are giving their patients clear information they will understand.

Excerpt 2

In order to identify and apply a leadership style, I established how it fits into the existing leadership architecture of my organization. Being an inspirational leader I was able to energize my team, create a new way of thinking and empowering. I also learned that giving power allows power to be returned to an individual through that very empowerment.

Excerpt 3

I had car trouble last week and went to my local garage, and came away with more than new tires. I observed – this shop treats their employees like family, and encourages everyone to achieve their full potential. They offered me a car to use while mine was in for repair – so they extended that same courtesy and respect to their customers. I had a strong sense that this company is successful because they are doing things right and going the extra mile. I learned that if you blend a culture of kindness and customer service into your organization, it will be returned tenfold.

Communicating Vision

Many of the courses in our curriculum stress the vital role an organizational mission and vision contributes to success, and so it was no surprise that many submissions incorporated commentary about these elements. The following PDSL submissions were selected because they share a different perspective of vision. The healthcare manager role is that of a generalist, and so we stress to students that they must have the big picture of what is occurring within their organization. One student highlighted the benefits of cross-training, and recognized it takes the whole organization to provide good patient care. Another example talks about the hard work of pushing a vision forward. They believed in a recommendation for department improvements, which took a long time to realize. Tenacity is a component of visioning. The final offering shares how believing in the vision and being able to tell the story are key ingredients to success.

Excerpt 1

Lifelong learning is the reason I love healthcare. One thing that my organization does is make each employee learn day to day tasks of the rest of the team. This way we will know the big picture of everyone's job and not just ours. Although I am in medical records, I had to learn what the intake department does, and also what billing does. I can now see that these other departments enable me to do my job, and vice-versa…we are all many parts to one great patient service.

Excerpt 2

I had an idea of where the linen carts could be placed in the ER to reduce the possibility of cross-contamination, and I pitched it to my supervisor. The initial idea did not get approved, but I kept the issue alive because I could see it was a problem spot. Later I proposed cabinets be installed in each ER room, and that idea was approved. I had a vision of how to solve a problem, and although not as quickly as I had hoped, eventually it was resolved.

Excerpt 3

In radiology new techniques and protocols are being discovered frequently. Our office had a chance to be trained on a new procedure by a leading prostrate radiologist, and I was asked to collaborate with some local urologists to secure patients to participate in a trial run. I was positive about the "vision" for these trials, and the promise the new procedure holds for future patients. It all went well, but then I found that I kept the message going as I followed up with patients to provide results, and keep them posted on the next steps.

Manage Change

Uncertainty with the status of the Affordable Care Act, the retailing of healthcare, and instability in the health insurance marketplace are but a few of the influencers that would cause any leader to seek additional training in change management. A study that examined how to build a leadership team of the future noted change as a topic of interest among health executives interviewed. Findings noted: "54 percent identified leading nontraditional health partnerships, such as joint ventures or strategic partnerships with payers and retailers, as a primary capability gap for their organizations, In addition, 48 percent of respondents identified community and population health management experience as a talent gap" (Health Research and Educational Trust 2014, p. 11).

Change is an inevitable fact of healthcare today, and our students were sensitized to it even more in our region because of local merger activity. PDSL submissions on leadership experiences associated with change addressed these local circumstances, but students also personalized their impressions of change. Key themes were flexibility and adaptability, creativity, and problem solving. One of the excerpts below demonstrates how one maternity ward was creative in response to an invasion of construction workers. Another passage reveals that sometimes the organization can be improved through change. The third offering shows that change is not static, and that to adapt to change requires problem solving techniques.

Excerpt 1

With the hospital expansion, my unit has had many changes lately, and our main goal has been to keep our patients safe throughout. We had to care for our patients while losing roughly half our rooms, so we used rooms on an adjacent wing to care for all the babies. There were also a lot of construction workers in and out. To differentiate the construction workers with special permission to be in our unit, we were creative and had baby feet painted on their safety helmets. Our team feels that we can handle any sort of change after this experience.

Excerpt 2

Our organization recently went through a huge change and expanded from hospice care only to respite and palliative care also. Being part of the new brand helped us to overcome a stigma some people associated with hospice, and signals hope and joy. Managing the new brand gives our organization a new meaning and focus on providing healthcare to the entire community.

Excerpt 3

At a recent staff meeting our scheduler shared that she was having a difficult time scheduling patients and I decided to evaluate how she was arranging for the providers who travel to the patient's home. The scheduler was using Map Quest and entering each individual patient's address each time a visit was needed. This was taking a great deal of time, so I researched a routing software that saves patients addresses, which will make it much more efficient. Now we are using a free trial of a routing system to see how it works, and likely will adapt it for the office. A leader seeks solutions and has to be innovative in problem solving.

Students were able to gain insight into some important lessons across the four sub-competencies of leadership. Self-assessment is an essential practice for leaders, and unless one knows their inner core they cannot know how they will respond when tested. Seeking new opportunities to grow takes leadership strength in and of itself, and so we tie this lesson to the PDSL activity. The handful of excerpts shared in this chapter represent a good cross-section of leadership traits, and because students had to record their experience, the hope is that they reflected on wisdom gained and will be able apply it when they are in a leadership role.

Leadership Competency: World Café Debrief

The World Café conversations about competencies have been referenced in previous chapters, and so readers will have a good understanding of how the debrief of participant findings represent a collective voice derived from three separate sessions. As shown in Table 5.1, comments on how students fulfill their leadership competency seemed to cluster around three areas: general skills of a leader, relating to people, and guiding the organization toward success.

Values-Driven Leadership Skills

As anticipated, general leadership skills appeared on the posting, such as time and stress management, delegation, and follow through. However, it was surprising to see skills related to core values. Students voiced respect for leaders who have taken time to self-reflect and know what their true north really is. They acknowledged respecting leadership that consistently follow their values. A cluster of words like humility, responsibility, moral grounding, ethics, and knowing where you stand supported this narrative. A final thread running through all three World Cafés was how a leader builds team through their actions. The "We not I" statement seemed to sum up this sentiment. Many times the inclusivity of having the leader working at the same level as the team is appreciated, but there are times when you need the leader to function above the team and be the liaison or buffer between the C-level and team.

Table 5.1   World Café Leadership Competency Debrief

Leadership Skills	Relating to People	Guiding Organization toward Success
• Ability to listen with understanding • Acknowledging mistakes • Being humble • Being responsible • Building work ethic • Continuing education • Critical thinking • Delegation • Don't be a boss, be a leader • Follow through • Going the extra mile • Guidance • Knowing where you stand • Lead by example • Moral grounding • Rewards • Open-door policy • Organization skills • Stress management • Taking initiative • Time management • We not I	• Able to apologize • Building trust • Emotional intelligence • Fairness • Good relationships • Keeping positive attitude • Listening skills • Maintain composure • Making someone feel comfortable • People skills • Relationship management • Self-control • Show enthusiasm	• Clarity of point/ purpose • Clear vision and goal • Coaching team • Cross-training • Keeping everyone on task • Know agency • Setting a course of action • Staying with the plan • Team building • Training the team

Relating to People

The 3 × 5 card with "emotional intelligence" (EI) written on it caused the cohort to pause and deliberate a bit longer on the meaning. Someone queried why the EI 3 × 5 card was not displayed under the leadership skills section. The table group that originated the idea was passionate that it remain under people skills because, as they pointed out, EI made the rest of the list under that category possible. Phrases like maintaining composure, self-control, and keeping a positive attitude are only feasible if an individual can be in control of themselves. Students see leaders as having the ability to do just that. Trust and fairness are also connected to an ability to hold one's own opinions or needs in check sufficiently in order to hear the other person's point of view. It was gratifying to see how such a short list of seemingly innocuous words could conjure up such heartfelt dialogue. Students were associating personal skills and potential success as future leaders.

The students are not alone in feeling passionate about the power of EI. It seems that EI is being incorporated into more leadership development curriculums, and this makes sense because interpersonal connections are essential to any transaction.

Guiding Organization toward Success

During debrief, everyone concurred that the dominant theme for guiding an organization toward success had to be teamwork. References directly related to teamwork appeared on 10 out of 13 – 3 × 5 cards that were posted under this banner. Coaching, training, setting a course of action, and keeping on task were all voiced as essential for any organization to thrive. One possible outlier was the card listing "know agency." As stated previously, the healthcare enterprise in our region was experiencing transition at the time the World Café sessions were held. One powerful comment germane to this posting was – *It's hard to know how to make the agency successful until we know where we are headed.*

The three overarching leadership competency themes emerging from the World Café debriefs indicate that a leader has to first complete self-reflection and requisite improvements before they can possibly lead a team successfully. Identifying and consistently following a set of core values is necessary to garner respect from a team, and a leader also has to be in control of their emotions in order to build trust, which is essential to being accountable for moving an organization ahead.

Students clearly articulated indispensable leadership competencies through both their PDSL submissions and World Café participation. Through both practices, students realized that they will have to groom these skills over time via experience. Building leadership strengths from a pre-career perspective provides a safe environment to stretch the boundaries of the possible with the support of faculty and peers.

Leadership Development: Promising Practices

Institute for Healthcare Improvement Open School for Health Professions

One promising student-centric practice is the Institute for Healthcare Improvement (IHI) Open School for Health Professions. IHI followed a hunch that students would want to learn through real-life and real-time opportunities through a common online platform. "In ten years, IHI has seen impressive growth: more than 700,000 students and residents have joined the Open School, more than 550,000 students and residents completed an asynchronous course, and more than 900 chapters have been created on college and university campuses in more than 90 countries" (Briddon et al. 2018, p. 73). One clear message the IHI "hunch" sends is that students are eager to learn and seek both the tools and opportunity to do so. Although the primary focus of IHI when it was founded over 30 years ago was quality improvement and safety, it has broadened to include leadership development as well. The authors challenge the healthcare workforce to invite the next generation to lead. Given the aging of the current healthcare workforce, this is excellent advice, and the IHI Open School presents an outstanding venue to do just that.

Customized Programs

Duke University created a customized approach to leadership development through the program, "Informed Mindfulness: the Power of Awareness and Choice in Effective Leadership." It makes perfect sense that a tailored program around mindfulness would be facilitated at Duke, as one of the most "well-recognized and evolved integrative centers in the country with a robust clinical program, integrative primary care practice and significant research program…and also one of the leading educators of health coaches in the country" (Hart 2014, p. 202).

The program is grounded on a premise that mindfulness will lead to awareness and better choices. "Leadership is not bestowed because of a title or role. It is a way of being. Leaders who foster self-directed behaviors clearly define expectations, speak openly about accountability, accept responsibility and ownership, empower others, evoke excellence, and bring about a learning environment with continuous improvement" (Aquilino et al. 2017, p. 20).

According to the National Center for Complementary and Integrative Health (2018), "Many Americans – more than 30 percent of adults and about 12 percent of children – use health care approaches developed outside of mainstream Western, or conventional, medicine. When describing these approaches, people often use 'alternative' and 'complementary' interchangeably, but the two terms refer to different concepts: If a non-mainstream practice is used together with conventional medicine, it's considered 'complementary.' If a non-mainstream practice is used in place of conventional medicine, it's considered 'alternative'. True alternative medicine is uncommon. Most people who use non-mainstream approaches use them along with conventional treatments. There are many definitions of 'integrative' health care, but all involve bringing conventional and complementary approaches together in a coordinated way. The use of integrative approaches to health and wellness has grown within care settings across the United States."

As integrative medicine continues to be recognized across the country, it will be important that clinician leaders honor the philosophical underpinnings of the practice. Ostensibly, an affinity is more likely to exist between program leadership, a vision for healthcare, and the very clientele the system is intended to serve. When a leadership program meshes seamlessly with an organizational culture, it is also more likely to be successful.

Appreciative Inquiry

Another promising practice similar to the affirming focus of mindfulness employed by Duke University is Appreciative Inquiry (AI). The AI method originated with a body of work in conjunction with the Cleveland Clinic decades ago by Dr. David Cooperrider of Case Western Reserve University in Cleveland, Ohio. Similar to the importance of posing appropriate questions and conversation at the core of World Café, inquiry is at the heart of AI. There are four "Ds" associated with the AI method. The first D is Discovery, which examines past and present success in order articulate the true core and possibility that exist within any organization. The second D is Dream, which is a visioning of what might be possible based on a past track record. The third D is Design, which generates prototypes of the possible and prompts participants to detail next steps to accomplish the objective. The fourth D is Destiny: what the best possible outcome looks like when fully executed.

Since its inception, the AI method has been applied across multiple sectors and has been adapted into affinity processes such as appreciative coaching and appreciative leadership. "Appreciative Leadership is the relational capacity to mobilize potential and turn it into positive power – to set in motion positive ripples of confidence, energy, enthusiasm, and performance – to make a positive difference in the world" (Whitney et al. 2010, p. 3). There is potential in self-reflection and decision making based on knowing core potential; this is a much needed leadership trait.

I earned the Appreciative Inquiry Certificate in Positive Business and Social Change through the Weatherhead School of Business at Case Western Reserve University, and was fortunate that the experience was under the tutelage of Dr. Cooperrider himself. Following the application of AI for my dissertation, I exercised the method spanning numerous projects. One initiative was a Leadership Development Series (LDS) for the American Red Cross, Ohio Chapter.

In the LDS course design, each phase of AI was paired with leadership skill development activities. In Session I, Discovery corresponded with Values-Driven Leadership; in Session II, Dream aligned with Visionary Leadership; in Session III, Design paired with Transformational Leadership; and in Session IV, Destiny was coupled with Authentic Leadership. The sessions were four hours in length, and held approximately every other month. The in-class format included lectures; individual, small and large group activities; and a take-home assignment. Between sessions, LDS participants modeled leadership skills with essential emergency management partners in home communities through the application of AI methods and access to technology. I served as the LDS facilitator and guided the cohort through a co-constructive meaning-making analysis during the in-class sessions. For example, core value statements revealed through Session I directed the visioning process in Session II. Through the 4D AI cycle, the project explored and validated value-based organizational indicators in order to foster deeper membership accountability. Leaders were guiding vision and mission based on a true assessment of potential. An overarching objective of the LDS was to boost accountability of leadership, and their teams as an extension, to fulfill emergency functions.

In order to ascertain if AI held the promise to groom transformational leaders, AI was introduced to students in a leadership class in a health administration program at a midwestern university. Students wrote vision statements, practiced self-reflection, provided AI coaching, and maintained professional portfolios. The course also referenced the "Leadership Challenge" work of Kouzes and Posner (2002, p. 13), who documented "when getting things done in organizations, leaders engage in these Five Practices of Exemplary Leadership: Model the Way, Inspire a Shared Vision, Challenge the Process, Enable Others to Act, and Encourage the Heart."

In order to document findings, students were administered a Leadership Practices Inventory (LPI), "containing the five subscales for each of the 'Five Practices for Exemplary Leadership' and...scores were significant for all five areas, the ones pertinent to this study were those that demonstrated vision, empowerment, and support of others" (Selcer et al. 2012, p. 16).

The Leadership Challenge tenets were also adopted by St. Vincent Hospital in Indianapolis, when they were faced with staff shortages, low personnel morale, and a possible takeover. As a faith-based institution, executives believed that there was a firm connection with the five practices, which would serve as the foundation for their BEST Initative. The acronym stands for "the best Budget, patient Experience, Safety, Team," and it was implemented systemically with great results. "While the previous role of leader was more akin to the management of tasks, not of leadership, what we have now is an environment in which we each take responsibility for the Five Practices every day – feedback – 77% reported that their leadership skills improved" (The Leadership Challenge n.d.).

Incorporating affirmative AI principles into a leadership development program holds tremendous promise because just like the mindfulness approach Duke University developed for their integrative medicine physicians, participants co-create a personalized approach to leadership. Leadership is grounded on meaning that the training promotes through self-reflection and visioning, and therefore it is more likely to have value for the originator. Whether executives at the Red Cross or students in a leadership development class, AI can certainly prepare leaders in their respective organizations.

Customization of proven models like the Leadership Challenge also hold great merit. Just like an academic program and a major hospital alike, each accessed the five practices model and employed the LPI to monitor impact.

Closing Thoughts

"There are over 480,000 books on Amazon related to leaders – and – organizations spend over $15 billion annually on different forms of leadership training and development" (Phipps and Prieto 2017, p. 56). But, when we cut through the staggering statistics, at the end of the day a leadership development program has to fit the needs of the individual, the team, and the institution charged with delivering outstanding healthcare.

Accountability has be the benchmark all leadership endeavors to achieve, because the healthcare discipline is responsible for improving the patient experience, philosophically transforming form a disease focus to wellness, and being the stewards of cost control. We can and must learn from the innovation of our peers and adopt, adapt, customize, or create leadership campaigns germane to our specific needs.

References

Aquilino, Michael, Horrigan, Bonnie, and Perlman, Adam. 2017. "Informed Mindfulness: The Power of Awareness and Choice in Effective Leadership." Accessed September 9, 2018. https://www.dukeintegrativemedicine.org/wp-content/uploads/2015/05/The-Power-of-Awareness-and-Choice-in-Effective-Leadership.pdf

Briddon, Michael, Strang, Carly, and Berwick, Donald. 2018. "Invite the Next Generation to Lead." *Healthcare Executive* 35(5): 72–2073.

Hart, Jane. 2014. "The Leadership Program in Integrative Healthcare at Duke University." *Alternate and Complementary Therapies* 20(4): 201–202.

Health Research and Educational Trust. 2014. *"Building a Leadership Team for the Health Care Organization of the Future."* Chicago, IL: Health Research & Educational Trust. Accessed September 9, 2018. http://www.hpoe.org/Reports-HPOE/leadership-team-future-2014.pdf

Herd, Ann, Adams-Pope, Brittany, Bowers, Amanda, and Sims, Brittany. 2016. "Finding What Works: Leadership Competencies for the Changing Healthcare Environment." *Journal of Leadership Education* 15(4): 217–233.

Kouzes, James, and Posner, Barry. 2002. *Leadership Challenge.* 3rd Edition. San Francisco: Jossey-Bass.

Leadership Challenge. n.d. "St. Vincent Hospital: Transforming a Culture to Become the Hospital System of Choice." Accessed September 9, 2018. http://www.leadershipchallenge.com/resource/st-vincent-hospital-transforming-a-culture-to-become-the-hospital-system-of-choice.aspx

National Center for Complementary and Integrative Health. 2018. "Complementary, Alternative, or Integrative Health: What's in a Name?" Accessed September 9, 2018. https://nccih.nih.gov/health/integrative-health#integrative

Ollier, David. 2018. "Achieving Accountability." *Physical Leadership Journal* 5(3): 18–23.

Phipps, Simone, and Prieto, Leon. 2017. "Why Emotional Intelligence Is Necessary for Effective Leadership: Know the Four Reasons." *Leadership Excellence Essentials* 34(6): 56–57.

Selcer, Anne, Goodman, Gerald, and Decker, Phillip. 2012. "Fostering Transformational Leadership in Business and Health Administration Education through Appreciative Inquiry Coaching." *Business Education Innovation Journal* 4(2): 10–19.

Stuart, Michelle, and Wilson, Carol. 2015. "Mentoring in Healthcare: A Rehabilitation Hospital's Launch of an Innovative Program for Emerging Leaders." *Healthcare Management Forum* 28(1): 4–7.

Whitney, Amanda, Trosten-Bloom, Amanda, and Rader Kae. 2010. *Appreciative Leadership: Focus on What Works to Drive Winning Performance and Build a Thriving Organization.* New York: McGraw Hill.

Chapter 6

Healthcare Professionalism Competency

Beyond Professionalism toward Interprofessionalism

The healthcare workforce is in transition, and is viewed more as an interprofessional team rather than just a single employee. The complexity of healthcare today is driving this concept, and it will require a rethink about how we frame professionalism going forward. For example, the Foundation for Medical Excellence launched the Organizational Professionalism Charter Project with four aims "patient partnerships, organizational culture, community partnerships, and operations and business...the charter is a clear and concise document, describing the principles of professionalism, that can remind leaders of organizational mission and accountability to the communities they serve" (Mason 2017). Inherent in this charter is the message that healthcare service delivery is not a solo act.

When we examine what skills will be necessary to successfully facilitate patient partnerships, a few logical abilities come to mind. Communication of course is top of the list, but this too can be expanded to include awareness of cultural sensitivity, and its accommodating practices. Engaging the patient and their support network as care partners would also include communication skills in advocacy, persuasion, and negotiation, and in order to advance the patient from entry through discharge, professionalism in time management, problem solving, and teamwork would be essential. The process is a relay, and every step of the journey requires each member to execute their part of the collective mission to the best of their ability.

The very concept of organizational culture conjures up collaboration, and it is this sum of the parts that can make or break an institution. Mission statements are commonplace in today's healthcare enterprise, and vision statements have transformed into action statements that permeate the organization. Professionalism comes into action as employees "walk the walk" and not just talk the mission. There is a need to exercise altruism, transparency, ethics, and a code of conduct in every function of one's job description.

In my public health tenure I have witnessed a shift in how organizations think about community partnerships, and this modification will alter professional skills that healthcare workers in all organizations will have to groom. One example is the requirement that hospitals conduct a regular community needs assessment. Whereas hospital personnel may not necessarily know where to begin to tackle this task, assessments are a routine component of public health work. A number of hospitals are indeed partnering with local health colleagues to accomplish the objective. Collaboration is necessary to complete projects and entails skills in navigation of group dynamics, communication, and resource sharing.

One of the more striking examples of community partnerships derives from the 2006 passage of the

Pandemic and All-Hazards Preparedness Act, which
charged health departments with planning and response
functions to incidents such as the influenza pandemic.
Public health personnel were trained in a series of
incident command courses offered through the Federal
Emergency Management Agency, and this greatly broadened
professionalism skill sets. Teams of employees were
responsible for cross-planning with first responders,
hospitals, law enforcement, and municipalities to establish
emergency operations centers, execute exercises, and
evaluate after action reports.

In order to execute operations and business accountably,
healthcare workers will have to exercise the utmost of
professional abilities. The very fact that confidentiality is
such an omnipresent requirement of the discipline requires
a conscious effort to honor privacy at all times. Functioning
with ethics, a code of conduct, and transparency are necessary
traits. Every member of an organization who touches a
medical record or billing statement will have to practice ethical
business principles because they are all components of the
organizational system.

An interesting research project conducted by the
Health Professions Council (HPC) to address professional
practice, arrived at a multi-dimensional construct of
professionalism. This multi-dimensional theory meshes with
an interprofessional description of professionalism. The
HPC studied three varied health professions: paramedics,
chiropodists/podiatrists, and occupational therapists. "Views
of professionalism did not diverge widely, regardless of
professional group. Rather than a set of discrete skills,
professionalism may be better regarded as a meta-skill,
comprising situational awareness and contextual judgement.
Organizational support, expectations of others, and patient
encounters were also factors" (Carter et al. 2015, p. 3).

The overlay of concepts like multi-dimensionalism and
interprofessionalism begin to describe the very environment

the healthcare workforce has to navigate in today's healthcare system. It is complex. A logical extension, therefore, regarding how we have to frame professionalism is that it has to be just as multifaceted. I especially liked the situational analysis component to of the HCS study because it implies a nimbleness that the employee can flex and adapt to as circumstances warrant. The term interprofessional also denotes an intentional, mutual, and reciprocal way of being and working.

Professionalism Competency: PDSL Insights

Readers are by now familiar with the PDSL portfolios students are required to compile each semester. A subtext to the PDSL narrative is that co-curricular activity is actually modeling professional behavior and cultivating the reality of lifelong learning inherent in the discipline. I believe that sending a consistent message of the worth of the practice has embedded within the students a sense of reward rather than obligation. Students are beginning to see the PDSL submissions as a component of their ongoing professional development. There are three sub-competencies under professionalism with fairly uniform submission rates: personal and professional accountability (32%), professional development and lifelong learning (34%), and contributes to the community and profession (35%).

Personal and Professional Accountability

Students reported accountability through decision making on the job. Two of the following excerpts demonstrate how students applied situational analysis before acting. This ability in an expression of professionalism, and the practice will be reinforced each time it is exercised with positive results. The third example speaks to the need for professionals to step outside their personal needs in order to be accountable to those they serve.

Excerpt 1

Working in bed control at the hospital I facilitate admissions, room changes, and expediting certain procedures. A patient came through the ER to have a C-section and from there was transferred to ICU; making two room changes to accommodate her needs. The patient was then downgraded and moved to a regular room. The next day an emergent situation came about and a nurse asked me to change her to yet another room so that a patient who kept falling could be moved closer to the desk to be routinely monitored. I asked her to select another patient to switch with because the new mother had already been moved too often. She disagreed with me. I appealed to the assistant director of nursing, and she agreed with me and felt in this situation that I had to be accountable to what I thought was right.

Excerpt 2

Working with certain patients over the years, I know there is always one who will ask a question and you are not at liberty answer it because it is not within your scope of practice. So as a healthcare professional I have learned to simply acknowledge the presence of the person and respond precisely that I simply cannot share that information, but you may ask my supervisor or the nurse in charge for that specific day.

Excerpt 3

When we are caring for others we often need to consider their perspective. We aim to provide the best quality of care we can to our clients daily. The truth of the matter is, our standard of quality may not be viewed the same as those we are servicing. We often look at things from the caregiver perspective, but what does our client see, and what do they say about the quality of care they receive? Unless you've been on the receiving end of care, you can never fully see things from a patient's point of view.

Professional Development and Lifelong Learning

Perhaps it is a difficult sell to tell students fully engaged in a rigorous program that they have to do more, learn more, and study beyond what the curriculum dictates. However, that is exactly the message that building a PDSL portfolio sends. A number of students come to our Bachelor of Science degree from a two-year clinical degree, and many maintain their certification or licensure, so the continuing education element of professionalism is not new to them. The following excerpts address the connection between professionalism and acquiring knowledge and staying current in the field.

Excerpt 1

I believe that there is always more to learn. To think that one knows it all is a brick wall in my opinion. This attitude prevents growth and feeds the ego. I received my certification from the Florida Certification Board about three years ago as a Behavioral Health Technician. Two years ago, I obtained the title of Certified Recovery Support Specialist. It is very important to me to keep learning, especially in the healthcare field. New approaches, theories, and technology are being discovered every day. This is not a field someone can afford to fall behind in. I am considering applying for my CAC (Certified Addiction Counselor) so I can be a bit more rounded in my field of study.

Excerpt 2

I attended a True Colors workshop to help personnel understand their personality and deal with personality differences of their teams. At first I thought this was going to be a silly experience, but I learned otherwise. It was an eye-opening experience. We are all so different, and it helped me better understand my co-workers. I am "blue", which is empathetic, compassionate, and sincere. I now know that we blues value relationship building, and I feel pretty good about that.

Excerpt 3

I am the one in my organization to train any new lab techs, and over these past few years I realize that I am good at it. I try to train them in a non-complicated manner by simply walking them through their job. I can see that following training they do their jobs well, and I feel that I had a small part of making that happen.

Contributes to the Community and Profession

The majority of students acknowledged the "feel good" return on investment that contributing to community and their profession provided for them. Some students perhaps volunteered for the first time, and were pleasantly surprised by how it made them feel. One class project turned into a life lesson about being open to learning opportunities.

Excerpt 1

Making contributions to the community and to one's profession shows participation in something bigger than oneself. It demonstrates that we are willing to help others in good times and in bad. I participated in a local festival and it taught me that helping others is great for creating lasting relationships and meeting great people from all walks of life.

Excerpt 2

Volunteering is helping in a couple of ways: helping me gain experience, and helping my community. Helping in my community is just a small step to bigger things. If everyone works together to make the community a better place, then there would be less negativity and violence. I feel more satisfied and have a better sense of self-worth.

Excerpt 3

For our class project a small group of us were going to make a video about bullying. We went to the park and were fortunate enough to see a group of teens there playing basketball, and they kindly participated in our video. We started to advocate with them and their parents about bullying and shared the shocking bullying statistics from Treasure Coast. We found out from the kids what they have been doing in their respective schools. One mentioned a specific situation in their school where someone was being bullied and others intervened. It turned out to be so much more than just a class assignment. Many of us had never been in that position before where we could educate others, and we want to repeat the experience in our careers.

Professionalism Competency: World Café Debrief

As shown in Table 6.1, students focused on three themes: accountability, appearance, and interpersonal skills. By far the interpersonal skills column drew the most attention. Across

Table 6.1 World Café Professionalism Competency Debrief

Accountability	Appearance	Interpersonal Skills
• Accountability • Actions speak louder than words • Do not burn bridges • Do your job • Find what works • Innovate • Meeting deadlines • On time/ punctual • Own up to your responsibility • Put the phone down • Stay up-to-date/ current • Time management • Watching what is said • Work ethic	• Attire – How you present yourself • Company parties • Company representative • Creating personal brand • Dress code • Dress for success • Email awareness • First impressions • Manners • Online footprint	• Apologizing • Be more direct/not wishy-washy • Behavior skills • Being a mentor • Being kind • Being open to criticism • Cultural awareness • Customer service • Emotional intelligence • Empathy • First – Be nice • Handling unprofessionalism • Keeping things light • Maintaining composure • Not making assumptions • Polite • Positive criticism • Respect • Say "I would rather, instead of no" • Show understanding • Social awareness • Soft skills • Speak clearly • Team player

all three World Cafés, everyone agreed that the best way to demonstrate professionalism is to work well with others.

Students acknowledged that accountability comes through in how one honors roles and responsibilities. Time management was described as not only being punctual and meeting deadlines, but also being timely by staying up to date on the latest trends. One 3 × 5 card posting that sparked a great deal of discussion was the phrase "put the phone down." One supervisor shared a story about a time an employee walked right into her because she was so engrossed in her phone. What type of message does this send to patients and colleagues alike?

Cards posted under the appearance banner included a list of the usual items such as dress for success, dress code, and first impressions. It was interesting to note in one of the World Café sessions that the need to create and maintain a personal brand was also deliberated. Personal brand includes dress and manners, but goes beyond that to consistently conduct business in a style that is all your own so that people come to expect how you will professionally respond in any given situation.

Students weighed in on the social media movement and how important it is to be cognizant of emails, Facebook, and what students called an online footprint. Social media is covered in a number of our courses, and so this was a nice crossover conversation to witness. The majority of our students are more focused on creating a LinkedIn page than boosting their Twitter accounts. Nevertheless, this was a timely discussion for students to have because "E-professionalism" training is needed beyond simple netiquette awareness. "In a national survey of accredited U.S. allopathic medical schools, 60% reported having incidents of students posting unprofessional content online. E-Professionalism…should include the development of professional values, actions, and aspirations (online behavior)" (Kaczmarczyk et al. 2013, p. 166).

Interpersonal skills was the theme under the professionalism competency with the most postings; there was a lot to say. An "emotional intelligence" thread ran through debrief with words like being more direct, being open to criticism, and maintaining composure. Students referenced the "personal brand" commentary shared earlier during the appearance report out.

Showing understanding, being kind, being nice, empathy, and cultural awareness were processed through the lens of interface with patients and clients. These professional behaviors mirror the skill to build patient partnerships mentioned earlier in the Organizational Professionalism Charter Project.

There were two postings that were intertwined: be more direct/not wishy-washy, and say I would rather, instead of no. Students noted that when supervisors exhibit these two behaviors it diminished their credibility, and in turn, their professionalism. A countermeasure to these ineffective practices is to have conviction of purpose and intent.

Professionalism seemed to have a number of affinity themes, and students concurred that it was likely that just one topic could suffice to describe the competency – interpersonal skills. They argued that accountability and appearance are embedded within their perception of a professional. Of course, there was no right or wrong opinion, just the fact that the discussion was taking place advanced the likelihood that professionalism was on the student's radar and would be incorporated into their career-readiness agenda.

Professionalism Competency: Promising Training Practices

Pre-Career Professionalism Training

As healthcare moves toward an interdisciplinary approach to care delivery, it makes sense for promising practices that groom professionalism to follow suit. One such practice resides in the University of Washington, which is home to six professional healthcare schools. They established a Center for Health Sciences Interprofessional Education in an effort to integrate and maximize training opportunities across the institution. "The course catalog for the University of Washington offers more than 50 collaborative interprofessional offerings for students in the health sciences...the existence of these course, and support for them, provides a platform from which students from diverse health professions can learn 'with', from, and 'about' each other outside their program 'silos'" (Bridges et al. 2011, p. 5). Students learn how to function as a team in order to deliver optimal patient care, and this framework will feel comfortable as students graduate and enter the healthcare workforce.

Another promising practice comes from the University of Memphis, with a three program approach to fostering professionalism. The innovative programs include "engaging public health students in professional skill development (Day One), interprofessional collaboration and systems thinking (Interdisciplinary Case Competition), and leadership in providing environmental support for health (Memphis Healthy U)" (Levy et al. 2015, p. S45). The intent on the Day One initiative was to prepare students for job entry immediately following graduation. Career readiness activities such as resume writing, improving oral and written communication skills, networking, and building business relationships were inclusive topics. The Case Competition formed a multidisciplinary team that would work collaboratively on an identified local health problem in order to build value for working with partners. The third component was "Memphis Healthy U," which enable students to directly work on health promotion projects across campus like tobacco free policy, bike sharing, or health fairs. The sum total of all three projects increased the likelihood that students would have the most comprehensive professionalism training and be ready to begin their health careers.

Professionalism through Case Competition

I can attest to the fact that the Case Competition approach to building professionalism works. During the 2017/2018 academic year our institution registered a team of students to compete in a regional case competition. The intent of the competition was to provide students with an opportunity to analyze and present a solution to real issues faced by healthcare organizations. In early January students across seven teams received the exact same case study to analyze, research, and prepare recommendations for advancing toward solutions. Each team was partnered with a local hospital, where a representative offered advice and coaching as necessary. Our team had an opportunity to shadow the CEO of our host hospital. We also attended a multi-departmental Lean Six Sigma project debrief. The team also presented a dry run of their project before an undergraduate class. This effort had a value added benefit of inspiring students to potentially participate in the competition the following year. The team prepared a report and presented their consultation before a panel of distinguished C-Suite judges. This was the inaugural participation for our institution, and even in competition with graduate-level programs our team won second place. Throughout the case competition students learned time and project management, research skills, team management, writing and public speaking, and confidence stretched with each skill acquisition. The peer-to-peer sharing of such an on-trend and vital assessment created a realization of what healthcare managers will actually do on the job.

Professionalism Training for Personal Care Aides

As healthcare needs and focus shifts, so too does the healthcare workforce and professionalism training requirements change along with the variations. One example comes from Washington State and their ongoing effort to re-balance state revenues toward in-home or community care rather than nursing home care. As a result of this state push, the Service Employees International Union of Washington State developed a Training Partnership for personal care aides (PCAs), the personnel pool largely responsible for at-home healthcare. "The Training Program began to field what would soon become the largest PCA training program in the country, annually serving more than 45,000 of the state's 60,000 PCAs. The program includes mentorship with seasoned aides, communication, problem solving, relationship, and cultural sensitivity to the patient" (Dawson 2016, p. 88). A well-trained and professional support workforce serves as an important component of the interdisciplinary team because they fill a niche along the continuum of care.

Institutional Values and Professionalism

A final promising practice comes from the American College of Physicians Foundation and the European Federation of Internal Medicine, which recommends integration of professionalism into the core values of an institution. Once professionalism is embedded and activated throughout the system it becomes a code of values that can be monitored through professional standard committees. The bottom line is that today's healthcare consumer is expecting a certain level of professionalism from their healthcare delivery system, and they have options of where they acquire the best service. A highly professional workforce committed to these principles will create greater patient trust and loyalty; deliver safer, higher-quality care; have less litigation and regulatory risk; manage resources more efficiently; practice in a consumer-centric manner; and work as a team in a consolidated manner (Anderson 2014, p. 28).

Closing Thoughts

Professionalism training is needed today to not only signal excellence for a savvy consumer base, but for the healthcare workforce themselves. If health personnel can realize the full potential of why they entered the discipline, they are more likely to sustain a career in healthcare. In order to reach such an objective, an ongoing focus on professionalism will have to trend in the field.

Starting with pre-career and early careerists, establishing venues to simulate the demands of the profession will be essential. Enabling opportunities for shared vision and mission, resource allocation, internal and external partnerships, modeling team work, and interprofessionalism will be the minimum training components. Treating health education programming as a dry run for the career to follow will likely increase the graduate's ability to hit the ground running.

Organizations will have to elevate professionalism into institutional values and mission statements in order to meet triple-aim benchmarks. Return on investment is bound to follow, realized in patient satisfaction scores and precious personnel pool retention, improved morale, and positive organizational culture.

References

Anderson, Dale. 2014. "Competing on Professionalism." *Trustee* (November/December): 26–28.

Bridges, Diane, Davidson, Richard, Odegard, Peggy, Maki, Ian, and Tomkowiak, John. 2011. "Interprofessional Collaboration: Three Best Practice Models of Interprofessional Education." *Medical Education Online* 8(16): 1–11.

Carter, Madaline, Hesselgreaves, Hannah, Rothwell, Charlotte, Campton, Paul, Burford, Bryan, McLachlan, and Illing, Jan. 2015. "Measuring Professionalism as a Multi-Dimensional Construct: Professionalism and Conscientiousness in Healthcare Professionals – Study 2 – Final Report for the HCPC." Durham University. Accessed September 22, 2018. http://www.hpc-uk. org/assets/documents/10005038Measuringprofessionalismasamu lti-dimensionalconstruct.pdf

Dawson, Steven. 2016. "The SEIU Healthcare NW Training Partnership in Washington State." *Journal of American Society on Aging* 40(1): 88–91.

Kaczmarczyk, Joseph, Chuang, Alice, Dugoff, Lorraine, Abbot, Jodi, Cullimore, Aime, Darymple, John, Davis, Katrina, Hueppchenn, Nancy, Katz, Nadine, and Nuthalapaty, Francis. 2013. "e-Professionalism: A New Frontier in Medical Education." *Teaching and Learning in Medicine* 25(2): 165–170.

Levy, Marian, Gentry, Daniel, and Klesges, Lisa. 2015. "Innovations in Public Health Education: Promoting Professional Development and a Culture of Health." *American Journal of Public Health* 105(S1): S44–S45.

Mason, Diana. 2017. "Professionalism in Health Care Organizations." *Journal of the American Medical Association* 317(12): 1203–1204.

Chapter 7

Healthcare Environment Competency

Healthcare Environment: Mirroring Societal Trends

The healthcare environment today is emerging with trends that mirror society. Just as civilization is wired through round-the-clock internet and instant messaging, so too has healthcare expanded their virtual resources such as telemedicine and virtual care. Changes in retail with an "add to cart" mind-set have shifted thinking about access to include healthcare at the corner drugstore. Standard healthcare job descriptions such as physician, nurse, and respiratory therapist now include new titles like patient navigator and community health worker. How the business of healthcare gets accomplished, where, and by whom represent changes in the healthcare environment. The healthcare workforce will have to be flexible, adaptable, and able to scale services to traverse this new playing field. In this new healthcare environment, patients will be viewed as consumers, partners, and co-creators of enterprise.

Virtual Healthcare

Remote locales that are underrepresented by medical personnel and facilities can benefit from telemedicine, which can satisfy the access gap. Underserved rural communities with perhaps just one general practitioner can seek second opinions on difficult cases through cable lines. Medium-sized communities with limited on-staff specialists can Skype into conference calls for next step recommendations on patient treatment plans.

Accessing technology in order for consumers to access healthcare is an important trend in healthcare. "A recent survey found eight of 10 hospital executives regard it as very or somewhat likely that by 2023 their organizations will have implemented telemedicine as a means of follow up with patients after their visits" (Winfield 2018, p. 2). If technology can assist with home visits to increase the likelihood that patients are compliant with treatment and prescription regimens, then re-hospitalization may not be as necessary. The upfront investment in technology may well be less than lost reimbursement for patient re-admittance. Healthcare organizations will have to be flexible in delivery modalities, and the healthcare workforce will have to adapt as well.

Retailing of Healthcare

In 2016 during an American College of Healthcare Executives presentation at the association's annual meeting, the keynote speaker commented on CVS, and how this retail drug store is taking on healthcare as we know it today. CVS is the "largest retail chain with more than 1,135 locations in 33 states – formed 70 partnerships with health systems – wants to be there to help with access, with more than 50 percent of the U.S. population living within 10 minutes of a Minute Clinic" (Stempniak 2016). Walmart and Walgreens are inline to echo this retail healthcare trend. In today's busy world, if consumers feel they can pick up a gallon of milk and get a flu shot at the same time, without an appointment and at a cost savings, then the decision is clear.

Creative adaptations of retail healthcare are ever-emerging. For example, a new twist on routine exams for student athletes or the school nurse can be satisfied with "cameras set up in schools in several local districts so that students can be seen without leaving school...Missouri based Cox Health runs five Walmart walk-in clinics – the majority of consumers (91%) who recently used a retail clinic reported they were satisfied or very satisfied" (Shute 2018, p. 1).

An emerging term for this untethering of healthcare services from hospitals is dubbed the retailing of healthcare. "It is no coincidence that retail medicine is taking off at a time when 77 million baby boomers are entering their senior years...they require increased access to health services, and location counts – urgent care clinics, ambulatory surgery centers, free standing emergency departments, and touch points like apps and kiosks" (Mason 2015, p. 4). Convenience, choice, and branding are always important elements in retail, and now count just as much with healthcare consumers.

Two other consumer-driven trends that are gaining traction and changing the healthcare environment are home-based diagnostics care and concierge services. With an ever-escalating profile of chronic health conditions, a niche market has emerged to provide home testing abilities for patients with diabetes, high blood pressure, or similar cases. Rather than standing appointments with a provider to monitor status, home-based diagnostics can accomplish the objective. Wireless capabilities allow patients to post and track data on a patient portal and providers can routinely assess conditions from a distance. "Primary care physicians may consider the patient's home an extension of the examination room, and home-based diagnostics is projected to reach $37 billion by 2021" (Shrank 2017, p. 389). Concierge care enables patients to place their doctor on retainer, and the contractual arrangement provides on-demand access. The elite services "typically charges $1,500 for highly personalized, round-the-clock access – but the physician still bills the patients insurance for services" (Shrank 2017, p. 388).

Changing Healthcare Workforce

In addition to brick and mortar changes, the healthcare workforce is also changing in response to shifting demands. The aging population has increased the mandate for care of a vulnerable population with complex and chronic care needs. "Healthcare spending on these high need adults is economically unsustainable; and 5 percent of these Americans account for 50 percent of the nation's healthcare spending" (Kaur 2016, p. 56). One effort to reduce the care burden is a new profession identified as community health workers, which is "recognized as part of a promising approach to help patients manage their own care, close gaps with clinicians, and reduce fragmentation among providers" (Kaur 2016, p. 57). Sometimes referred to as outreach, engagement, or care management workers, there is currently no uniform position description or certification standard for these individuals. Although some Medicaid reimbursement may be applicable for their function, many of these workers are funded through grants or temporary revenue cycles, which further test the stability of the job.

The quest for patient safety still drives the healthcare environment, and this too can be scaled to meet demand. One of the original objectives derived from the Institute of Medicine's *To Err Is Human* report focused on prescription underuse, misuse, or overuse. Shining a light on the important role of pharmacist is becoming one of the latest healthcare trends. "Incorporating pharmacist into physician group practice or accountable care organizations to monitor patients with chronic diseases and their medications between appointments can contribute significantly to improving outcomes and controlling costs – turf issues tend to subside in team based models"

(Kreimer 2018, p. 24). Reformatting what teams used to look like in the healthcare environment to include new partnerships benefits not only the patients, but the workforce as well.

There appears to be a direct link between the shifting healthcare environment that is driven by both consumer needs and the system's response. As consumers seek quality of care at a convenient locale with the best price, so too the healthcare enterprise adapts to fulfill demand within the triple aim triangle. Patient safety, quality, and cost are realistic drivers for both parties in this movement. Engaging patients and clients as partners to co-create new ways of doing business will likely result is a custom-built system that satisfies both.

Healthcare Environment Competency: PDSL Insights

As we continue to explore changes in the healthcare environment, we can review four specific sub-competencies under the healthcare environment competency. For the 2017/2018 academic year when students were required to report under sub-competencies, the patient's perspective garnered the most responses (34%), followed by healthcare personnel (32%), community and the environment (21%), and healthcare systems/organizations (14%). Many of our students have a clinical background and are currently working in direct patient care as they pursue their advanced degree in healthcare management. Therefore, it is not too surprising that the patient perspective sub-competency rated first in submissions.

Patient's Perspective

The following four excerpts from students PDSLs have a theme of awareness and compassion throughout. Being aware of how the treatments and services provided impact on patients is essential to maintaining an excellent quality of care. Experiencing the same treatments as a patient rather than provider sensitizes us to the human side of the industry.

Excerpt 1

At the mental health agency where I am currently employed the method of healthcare delivery is person-centered service. This has changed my perspective to view the "patient" as a person not as a "diagnosis" or as "a mentally ill person." Tending to them from the moment they walk in to the waiting room with a greeting and a smile has many times been just what the client needed.

Excerpt 2

I am a CNA and do patient care. One of our patients was a little French woman who could not speak the language. Her daughter said she is really a "girly girl", and I thought about that. The next day I brought in some nice lip balms, gave her a manicure, and applied lotion to her dry skin. She was thrilled and always happy to see me after that, even though she did not know English – we communicated. Getting that patient's perspective was a valuable experience.

Excerpt 3

Recently I injured my back, and working in radiology, my boss suggested I get an MRI just to check things out. I set up the appointment at an office where I used to work. Normally, I am used to seeing the MRI technologist being uptight, especially if things do not go right. But my technician was calm, and he made me feel better even though I am very claustrophobic. Getting this patient's perspective on my own type of work made me love working in radiology even more that I already do.

Excerpt 4

I attended a seminar about breast cancer to gain more information about the myths, truths, and treatments, I felt this experience fell under the patient's perspective competency because as a healthcare manager it is important to have empathy and understanding for patients as they undergo hardships in their lives. While this is usually something for clinical personnel as a healthcare manager, you may encounter these patients and it is important to be familiar with what the patient may be going through.

Healthcare Personnel

As expected, a number of submissions around the healthcare personnel sub-competency focused on job descriptions for various positions. Students seemed to exercise their PDSL assignment to explore possible career options. The following excerpts were selected because they shed light on how the healthcare workforce are likely to seek compatibility with their skills and organizational placement. There is also a reference to the generalist nature of the healthcare manager position, and the need to gain the big picture of organizational operations in order to be able to navigate systemically.

Excerpt 1

I started off in physical therapy, where I helped patients gain mobility. From there I went on to obtain my CNA certification and worked in home health. I later joined our army and served as a combat medic, receiving EMT training along the way. Following discharge from the army my PT CEO hired me back into the practice. All these skills are building to where I am now – training to become a healthcare manager. I know that this vast healthcare experience will make me a better professional and member of the healthcare workforce.

Excerpt 2

I signed up to go to a lecture on PET/CT scans. I think it is important to continually grow in your education no matter what field you are in. Even as an administrator it is important to know the clinical aspects of the job as well. Although I am not part of radiology, I always like to know the basics and how these different types of tests differ and how they can benefit the patients. As a manger, you must know every aspect of the field in order to manage it in a knowledgeable manner and know how to be fair to all the employees under your wing.

Excerpt 3

To better understand the need for healthcare personnel within a large health system I interviewed an HR Manager with over 16 years of experience. She was an excellent source of information about each department and position. We discussed the degree I am pursuing and my classes, and what career paths would work. I came away with a personalized plan to reach my career goals.

Excerpt 4

Our Human Resources department was conducting surveys to see how they might change the new hire orientation process. I shared that I felt the night shift personnel sometimes get overlooked. They display all the same values and personal integrity as the day shift does, but very often feel left out when it comes to the organizational story. When I saw the new manual, she had taken some of my suggestions into consideration. These changes will go a long way to improving morale.

Community and the Environment

There was a clear and uniform theme under the community and environment sub-competency. Institutions benefit from outreach to their communities through special events and demonstrations of civic support. Students are involved in health fairs and annual events as an extension of their current employer, but they seek extra-curricular opportunities on their own as well.

Excerpt 1

My current employer offers several community health fairs throughout the year. I participated in registering our male citizens during a free prostrate exam event. We provided complimentary lab testing, provided education, and follow results through their personal physicians. The hospital earns the respect and admiration of those involved through this free service, and also earns a good reputation. I was able to be part of a community outreach, and also meet new people outside my department.

Excerpt 2

My organization is really into community events, and we host a Christmas parade and the big air show annually. My supervisor always makes it clear that she wants us to participate in these events because it builds relationships with other business in the area, and potential patients may get to know us too. In addition to these two events, we drive patients to appointments, and have a big RV that we can hold free flu clinics from. I can see that it all ties together

*because it signals that we care and are here to serve –
in good and difficult times.*

Excerpt 3

*I went to an event in our area that was a ground
breaking for a new veteran's facility. I have always
been curious and wondered why our veterans get
such poor healthcare. It actually makes me a bit sad
because I have a number of family members who have
served. I was so glad I went because I can see that
there were a number of citizens that feel the same as I
do, and perhaps together we can make some changes.*

Healthcare Systems and Organizations

The health systems and organizations sub-competency had
the lowest PDSL entries, at an average of 14% across two
semesters. It seems apparent through the following excerpts
that systems and healthcare organizational structures
overall are areas our students are motivated to understand
better. The only way to gain knowledge is to ask questions
and seek the answers. One class event, which hosted a
crossover session with our EMS program, met the intended
objective.

Excerpt 1

*Our class interfaced with our EMS students during a
class exchange, and I learned just how interconnected
our services are. I was aware of the clinical side of the
arrangement, but did not understand the managerial
issues such as how patients might have to pay for
ambulance services. A lot of issues were unwrapped
and I now know the political side of the partnership as
well. Healthcare is really multi-dimensional, but we
are all part of the same system.*

Excerpt 2

I have kept an open mind to the possibility that each hospital may hold different ideals than that of the hospital in which I work. Recently I had the chance to attend a presentation and tour of another hospital in this region. I honed in on the main goal of the lecture: improving patient satisfaction with their care givers. The presentation opened my eyes to the fact that even though I work for another hospital, we are all in the same community trying to improve exceptional healthcare for our community's loved ones. This presentation has motivated and inspired me to become more involved in our healthcare community.

Excerpt 3

I attended a presentation on our hospital expansion. Previously I had assumed that the decision was solely based on economics. The speaker detailed how population, demographics, and positioning of other hospitals in this region factored into the decision. I gained insight in to what a team decision this really is and it is not just about money. I was glad I went to the session and learned more about how healthcare functions.

Healthcare Environment Competency: World Café Debrief

Students discussed three main themes under the healthcare environment competency which related to the patient's perspective, seeking understanding about the various systems throughout the healthcare enterprise, and teamwork. As shown in Table 7.1, the following lists include words that reflect the student's voice.

Table 7.1   World Café Healthcare Environment Competency Debrief

Patient Perspective	Healthcare Systems	Teamwork
• Bedside manner • Clear up confusion • Compassion • Empathy • Faith (during illness) • Helping patients with insurance • Hippocratic Oath • Listening • Relate to patient's view • Response rates/timing	• Compliance • EPIC System • External partners • Financial systems • Information management • Inter-departmental communications • Learn health roles • Mergers • Mission statements • Organizational culture • Organizational systems • Recovery center • Rehabilitation services • Role of "front desk" • Remote satellites	• Cross-training • Internships • Huddles • Job shadowing • People skills • Programming demands • Quick thinking • Resource allocation • Staffing • Teamwork • Time management • Writing skills

The patient's perspective sub-competency seemed to be the most straightforward dialogue. To a participant, there was consensus that compassion and empathy were called for, and a polished bedside manner is essential. An explanation of one 3×5 card with the word "faith" seemed to prompt students to weigh in. A number shared that faith is important to patients and their families during illness, and they linked it into cultural awareness.

Specific terms under the healthcare system sub-competency derived from the joint World Café session with students and healthcare professionals. For example, the EPIC system garnered a substantial conversation during debrief. Participants saw merit in the system, but some students working in smaller offices noted frustration voiced by their administration.

Generally, students recorded a need to learn more about organizational culture and systems, especially outside their immediate departments.

Under the teamwork banner, 3 × 5 cards acknowledged staff as a resource, and the need to maximize the asset. For example, cross-training would help with succession planning. A few students were keenly aware of this need because at the time of the World Café, our region in Florida had just experienced a hurricane. Staffs were stretched thin both during and immediately following the incident. Personnel had to assist colleagues where needed, and valuable lessons were learned. The term resource allocation was directly linked to an identified need.

Healthcare Environment Promising Practices

Environmental Stewardship

Similar to consumer drivers of convenience, cost, and access that are shifting perceptions of healthcare today, so too is an elevated environmental consciousness directing the course. One promising practice in this trend comes from the state of Ohio, which is leading the United States in energy star hospitals. The Ohio Hospital Association's Energy and Sustainability Program worked directly with "Practice Greenhealth" to profile success strategies of six hospitals in the state.

A wide array of initiatives represent the creativity and impact of making simple changes that add up to a positive environmental footprint. For example, the 88th Medical Group at Wright-Patterson Air Force Base in Dayton salvaged doors, windows, and lights from a recent renovation and donated them to the Montgomery County Habitat for Humanity. These items did not just end up in the landfill. The Louis-Stokes Cleveland VA Medical Center formed a Green Team to increase renewable energy, use safer chemicals, and enact a sustainable requisition and purchasing protocol. These changes were made possible by implementing an organizational culture change toward going green.

Mercy Health in Youngstown reduced pharmaceutical waste and lead poisoning in children. They promoted a culture of system-wide energy efficiency. The University Hospital in Cleveland worked with local stakeholders to encourage a reduction in automobile use and a healthy biking lifestyle. The bike share "UH Bikes" is in cooperation with both Cleveland and Cuyahoga Counties. The hospital also launched "antimicrobial stewardship" through use of triclosan-free soap. A common thread through the biking and hand soap campaigns is the dual value of improved healthcare and environmental thoughtfulness.

The Mt. Carmel system, comprised of six hospitals throughout the greater Columbus area, formed a "Green Team." "Recycling efforts at Mount Carmel East in just one year have saved the equivalent of 2,298 barrels of oil, reduced the equivalent of 386.4 metric tons of Greenhouse Gas emissions, resulting in a Net Energy savings of 7,573.5 British Thermal Units and saved the equivalent of 3,463 trees" (Ohio Hospital Association 2017, p. 14). The lesson learned from this group was to communicate in a way that colleagues understand – tell the story and make it compelling. I believe that the stats from just one hospital for one year do just that.

Preparedness Planning

I recall working directly with All-Hazards Preparedness mandates in 2011 when an EF-5 tornado hit the city of Joplin, Missouri. Directly in the aim of that disaster was Mercy Hospital.

Once the dust settled and there was time for reflection and acknowledgment of lessons learned, I remember having the privilege of participating in a national Medical Reserve Corps workshop in Washington, DC, that was led by John Farnen, Mercy's Executive Director for Strategic Planning. The stories of heroism, quick thinking, altruism, community partnerships, and plans to rebuild have remained with me.

"The decision to evacuate was evident and immediate. Mercy Hospital Joplin evacuated 183 patients, including 28 critical care patients in addition to numerous staff and visitors also in the facility within 90 minutes following the tornado – responsibility for patient care did not stop once the patients were safely evacuated" (Missouri Hospital Association 2012, p. 17). In order to accomplish the seemingly impossible, the Mercy team relied on their internal environmental systems and strong support from long-standing and well-established community partnerships.

In the wake of the disaster help poured in from across the nation. I remember one story Mr. Farnen shared about the delivery of shipping containers that were used for temporary ER and exam rooms. Once these units had served their purpose, they were recycled to build satellite clinics in areas of underserved Missouri. What a terrific example of environmental stewardship and creative application of resources.

The Joint Commission on Resources has published a compilation of lessons learned from the Joplin experience, and it is well worth a read. The theme of the publication is that it pays to prepare. pre-planning is essential of course, and consideration of communication channels, resource and asset allocation, utilities, and medical surge are addressed. Staffing capacity and management of spontaneous volunteers have to be considered and exercised long before an event occurs. The next chapter in the Mercy Hospital story is equally inspiring. Rebuilding plans were implemented with safety and environmental stewardship in mind. Tornado impact windows are just one example of learning from past experience and making improvements for potential future events.

Healthcare Workforce: Reinventing Careers

As new positions, roles, and responsibilities spring up in the healthcare environment, the healthcare workforce also has an opportunity to reinvent careers to meet the shifting landscape.

> With the digital shift, health systems will begin to employ chief digital officers, digital strategists to monitor changing communications trends, innovation specialists, and, most importantly, programmers who will work on continually improving their organization's digital platforms, including the integration of telemedicine and mobile healthcare options. (Self 2016, p. 59)

The emergence of virtual healthcare, telemedicine, and retail medicine are driving new career options. Increasingly, personnel may be untethered from the hospital and working in patient homes or embedded with health organizations as members of a community interdisciplinary team. It is understandable, therefore, that a new approach to career-building and growth would have to follow an innovative path. Is the existing healthcare system geared up for this new career model? This reality needs to be remedied for the human resource component of the healthcare environment to meet demands of healthcare reform.

Innovation is needed to pilot a healthcare career course. Competency development and growing critical thinking, problem solving, technology, and interpersonal skills will be minimum requirements. Academia should encourage opportunities for students to gain career insight and understanding well ahead of a pending graduation date. Organizations should foster cross-training, team building, community partnerships, and reward creativity.

Closing Thoughts

We have to consider the healthcare environment as more than stationary concrete structures and more than just a static system resigned to business as usual. The rise in consumerism, connectivity of wireless systems, responses to increasing disasters, and trends yet to be identified require a new vision.

Traditional healthcare workforce titles exist, but should not feel threatened by the dichotomy of new roles and job descriptions. Change is possible, and whether it is environmental stewardship or preparedness partnerships, healthcare is agile and will adjust.

References

Kaur, Manmeet. 2016. "Community Health Workers: Birth of a New Profession." *Generations, Journal of the American Society on Aging*, 40(1): 56–63.

Kreimer, Susan. 2018. "Coordinated Value." *Physician Leadership Journal*, 5(4): 20–24.

Mason, Scott. 2015. "Retail and Real Estate: The Changing Landscape of Care Delivery." *Frontiers of Health Services Management*, 31(3): 3–15.

Missouri Hospital Association. 2012. "Preparedness and Partnership: Lessons Learned from the Missouri Disasters of 2011: A Focus on Joplin". Joint Commission Resources: 1–36. Accessed September 30, 2018. https://www.jointcommission.org/assets/1/6/Joplin_2012_Lessons_Learned.pdf

Ohio Hospital Association. 2017. "Ohio Healthier Hospitals: A Collection of Environmental Leadership Case Studies." Accessed September 30, 2018. https://ohiohospitals.org/OHA/media/Images/Membership%20Services/Energy/EnergyProgramcasestudiesbooklet2017.pdf

Self, John. 2016. "The Impact of Healthcare Transformation on Career Paths." *Healthcare Executive*, 31(4): 56–59.

Shrank, William. 2017. "Primary Care Practice Transformation and the Rise of Consumerism." *Journal of General and Internal Medicine*, 32(4): 387–391.

Shute, Debra. 2018. "What's Next for Healthcare? Part 1." *Healthcare Leadership Review* 37(4): 1–5.

Stempniak, Marty. 2016. "5 Implications for Hospitals Now That Retail in Health Care's New Front Door." Hospital and Health Networks. Accessed September 30, 2018. https://www.hhnmag.com/articles/7048-five-implications-for-hospitals-now-that-retail-is-health-cares-new-front-door

Winfield, Lia. 2018. "Responding to a Changing Healthcare Environment." *Healthcare Financial Management* (May): 1–3.

Chapter 8

Business Skills Competency

Business Skills Competencies: Agile and Adaptable

The business of healthcare is multi-faceted and includes strategic planning, financing, marketing, organizational development, governance, quality improvement, and a few more specialties. Two key elements keep the system humming along: technology and the healthcare workforce. Technology is driving how business is conducted, and in order to keep pace, today's healthcare workforce will have to hone business skill competencies that are agile and adaptable.

Technology

Faced with workforce shortages, an aging workforce population, and increasingly customized roles and functions, it seems both logical and inevitable that technology could fill some gaps. Thomas (2018) notes "labor accounts for almost 60 percent of noncapital cost" in healthcare, and so the term "no-collar workforce, a combination of humans and machines that results in enhanced performance and drives greater efficiencies" was coined. Four distinct types of technology are currently in play. Robotic process automation manages basic and repetitive tasks, and intelligent cognitive automation can ease ongoing tasks like inventory control. Machine learning is yet another step up that can actually anticipate needs and respond to an array of situations to arrive at best outcomes, while artificial intelligence is the top of the ladder with an ability to problem solve and self-activate as necessary.

Healthcare is no exception to a hyper-connected workforce. The key is to use technology to benefit workflow. For example, some healthcare enterprises are not fully equipped to manage the mounting IT demands, and so "healthcare IT outsourcing will increase by 7.6 percent a year, reaching $50.4 billion by 2018, up from $35 billion in 2013" (General Dynamics Health Solutions 2015, p. 21). By outsourcing complex systems, administrators can focus on how best to apply the data analysis the system provides.

Given this new reality, the author recommends that C-suite executives will have to pay attention to technology and acclimatize their organizations to reap the benefits. Recommendations include designing work stations with tech options, accessing collaborative platforms for strategic planning and data management, and fostering a tech-savvy workforce. Risk policies will also have to be crafted to mitigate and treat the possibility of tech abuse.

Along with the benefits of technology, threats are very real. "In 2015 nearly half of healthcare providers – 47% – said their data had been compromised...the average cost of a data breach for healthcare organizations is over $2.2 million...72% of malware attacks in 2016 were caused by ransomware" (Roemer 2017, p. 10). A cybersecurity focus is quickly becoming an integral component of any organizations objectives.

With the expansion of public health information and E-information, safeguarding HIPPA regulations, and a growing online presence of both patients and providers, organizations

are looking for options to use technology safely. Cloud
computing may pose a solution to technology protection
and optimal application in three ways. "Better flexibility with
spending – you are using services on demand…you want
your operations to move as smoothly as possible – cloud is
optimized for scalability, and interoperability is a key concern
of healthcare that is furthered by cloud environments"
(Puranik 2018, p. 28).

As technology is integrated into the work functions and
workforce of healthcare, it is no wonder that the American
Hospital Association (AHA) hired a former FBI veteran to
serve as their cybersecurity advisor. As a component of the
AHA Center for Health Innovation, an informative flyer was
developed that highlights 12 considerations that CEOs should
consider as they investigate and address cybersecurity in their
institutions. Establishment of both risk-mitigation and incident
response plans were among the recommendations. Given the
startling data about malware and ransomware trends, these
are indeed timely suggestions. One overarching proposition
raises the objective of building a cybersecurity culture within
the organization. "Knowing that the people of the organization
represent the best defense against cyber threats or the greatest
vulnerability, do we have a proactive top-down culture
of cybersecurity, in which every leader and staff member
believes he or she has a duty, a role and the power to defend"
(Riggi 2018).

Human Resources

Agility is required in seeking, training, and optimizing the
best talent in any organization, and healthcare is no exception.
According to Platonoya and Hernandez (2013, p. 290),
"Personnel compensation accounts for about 60%–85% of the
operating budget in a typical healthcare organization" and
based on a national study, three human resource strategies are
associated with overall institutional planning: "finding talent in

advance for key job openings, stressing organizational culture and values in the selection process, and basing individual or team compensation on goal-oriented results" (Platonova and Hernandez 2013, p. 290).

One example of the successful implementation of human resources and organizational strategy comes from the Cleveland Clinic revenue cycle training department. An institution as large as the Cleveland Clinic has a tremendous need for talented employees, and their onboarding process is 90 days long. The finance department launched a program called "learning paths," which was a combination of job aids and both classroom and online sequential learning modules. Profiles of staff already in finance roles were readily available with their photo and job descriptions. As the program progressed, interest was expressed from staff outside the finance department, and participation increased. A job-shadowing component was added to the "learning paths" initiative to broaden the scope of learning about other roles within the organization. Overall the impact of the program has been positive, with "10 percent of participants joined to gain better understanding of their role, 23 percent enrolled in a technical, college, or university as a result of their job shadowing experience, 13 percent were offered a job in the department they shadowed, 36 percent chose to remain in their current job roles" (Djukic 2015, p. 80).

These are both challenging times and invigorating times for healthcare, and we just have to remain open to opportunities that may arise. Imagine possibilities in the synergy of a talented workforce interfacing with appropriate business technology. Flexibility will be needed as the workforce adapts to new products, processes, and procedures. Ours is not a static discipline, and we cannot remain entrenched in old systems, albeit tried and true. Agility will need to be added to our skills, as we will have to be nimble in responding to higher expectations for quality of care by the health consumer.

Business Skills Competency: PDSL Insights

The business skills competency has the largest number of sub-competencies with eight. During the 2017/2018 academic year, students submitted sub-competency comments to their PDSL portfolios. Under business skills, the sub-competency with the most submissions was quality improvement (21%), followed in second place by general management (16%), third place was risk management (15%), fourth place was financial management (13%), a tie for fifth place with human resources and information management (11%), sixth place was strategic planning and marketing (9%), and in seventh place was organizational dynamics/governance (7%).

Quality Improvement

Students expressed their experiences in quality improvement (QI) mainly through the lens of their current roles in healthcare. Many witnessed a process or protocol that could be tweaked for improvement. The following two excerpts were selected because they demonstrate a preemptive action for quality improvement and a connection between a good business model and QI.

Excerpt 1

I was going to volunteer for a non-profit that was offering an annual free dental clinic. I thought before I do this I should shadow the dental clinic for a while so I would be well aware of how they function. I learned that they prepare ahead of the day because they expect large crowds. I helped with sterilizing instruments and preparing trays. By helping these professionals, I learned the skills to manage risks by overseeing obstacles before they could possibly arise.

Excerpt 2

This semester I have done a lot of research on quality improvements because my goal is to have my own physical therapy business one day. Of course I want to improve the quality of the actual therapy, but also every other aspect of the patient experience. This includes when the patient begins with travel to the office right through to how well they understand the therapeutic plans.

General Management

PDSL submissions under the general management sub-competency related largely to interpersonal skills. People skills tended to be reported on more than any business model or technical skill. The following two quotes demonstrate a clear connection between keeping an agency running smoothly and a paying attention to human resources.

Excerpt 1

I implemented weekly meetings in my office: Thursdays with staff, and then Mondays with the physicians. I wondered if staff would like to take over running their meetings, and so surveyed them about it, and everyone was interested. Now I can concentrate on other office operations. I am also keeping an eye on who might be a manager-in-charge in my absence.

Excerpt 2

As a healthcare manager I always like to make sure my employees feel appreciated. I implemented Thankful Tuesdays, where another manager or myself write a letter, buy a little something sweet for the staff, or make an announcement about what a great job they are doing. It does not go unnoticed.

Risk Management

A number of the risk management PDSL submissions referenced prevention of slip and falls or examples of mitigation of trauma. The following citations examine risk management from a holistic perspective, and reveal the systemic benefits of well-practiced situational analysis to potential hazards.

Excerpt 1

This year I had the chance to participate in an emergency preparedness situation at my job when Hurricane Irma came through Florida. I got to see firsthand how the chain of command in such a large system works, how it changes during and after a disaster. It was really amazing to watch leadership guide an entire hospital system through an emergency and it made me aware of the business skills, planning, and amount of work that goes into preparing for such an event. I learned what it takes to keep a hospital running through a natural disaster.

Excerpt 2

In working in the ER I noticed that it may take a couple of days to get labs back on patients. I decided to automatically put any patients entering the ER on "contact precautions" until the clean test results come through. This simple act has lowered the risk of spreading infections like MRSA, not only for patients, but also staff.

Financial Management

The theme that tended to run through financial management PDSL submission was creativity. Students experienced opportunity in their current placements to simplify a financial process, reduce remittance turnaround times, or save the institution money. The following excerpts provide examples of the latter.

Excerpt 1

Working with home health patients, supplies are constantly being ordered. There was a time when nurses just accessed the supply room and took what they needed. During a quarterly meeting we heard about a change in policy. Supplies would be ordered by supervisors and mailed directly to patients' homes. Many of the staff thought this was ludicrous, and would make their jobs harder. However, when we found out how much the company was losing by having such a one-ended policy, we accepted it. I now order what I need two weeks ahead of time, and only what I need.

Excerpt 2

Made a discovery that 250 ml saline bags would serve our clinic needs, and they were much more cost affordable than the 500 ml bags we were ordering. Just this simple observation and change I know will be cost-effective in the long run, and reduce our purchasing budget.

Human Resources Management

It was a bit surprising that the human resources management sub-competency rated fairly low, in a tie for fifth place at just (11%). Over the years, a number of our students have expressed interest in human resources as a career choice, and several alumni are currently working in that area of healthcare. The following quotes highlight that students are still in exploration mode where human resources is concerned.

Excerpt 1

*This past November one of my neighbors went on
maternity leave after she had her first child. It was so
inspiring to hear her describe the experience she had
with her human resources department. She stated
how they provided a brief overview of the policies
and procedures and helped her fill out forms. With
so many constant changes in healthcare, overall
she was happy to say she was provided with the best
experience an employee can ask for. This was such
an inspiration for me and made me realize I'm on the
right track with my career. My goal is to become the
best healthcare manager I can be, and one day have
someone feel the way my neighbor did about me and
my team.*

Excerpt 2

*Last year our company was preparing for the DCF
inspection for continuation of licensure, and I was
asked to help with organization of the HR files. I
learned so much about policy and procedure, and
the standards expected for keeping files in order. I
also learned to honor confidentiality, as the files I had
access to were those of my colleagues.*

Information Management

Similar to the creativity aspect of business that students
voiced under the financial management sub-competency,
information management was also peppered with examples
of innovation. The following excerpts express how students
frame information as more than just big data management
systems; social media and appropriate applications are also
relevant.

Excerpt 1

I volunteered to be a member of a local coalition with our health department. Perhaps it was just because I am a millennial, but I was put in charge of the social media campaign. I have been tracking the uptick in hits to our site, and feel really good to report back to the committee on our success.

Excerpt 2

When I started working at the preschool I noticed staff were watching the children and also trying to do appropriate record keeping with signing children in and out – it was a bit strenuous. I created a list of all the students, with a column for their parents/guardians who were authorized to pick them up, and put it all on an iPad. Now, at the end of the day, this busy time runs smoothly because we just have to check the column and initial. We also have a data run if we need it of pickup times and who might consistently run late.

Strategic Planning and Marketing

One of the more interesting strategic planning submissions was submitted by a student not currently working in the field. She accurately applies an experience from her volleyball team. An example of marketing is provided to showcase how students make connections between coursework and the co-curricular PDSL requirement.

Excerpt 1

Before every game we have a spreadsheet on how to defeat our opponent. On the spreadsheet we have strategies for all components of the match, defense and offense, and for what the opponent might try to do against us. We plan ahead for all the games for the best outcome. Someday in the future as a healthcare manager I will have to apply these tactics as my business skills.

Excerpt 2

Our dental office really did not have a marketing campaign, so I suggested to my boss that I could lead that effort. I really investigated how to go about this, and tried a few things. Then I registered for the marketing class, and got some solid tips. My co-workers were surprised that after a few months our patient roster has doubled. I am so stoked to keep pushing out our practice name and the services we offer, and will not think twice the next time before trying new things.

Organizational Dynamics/Governance

The organizational dynamics/governance sub-competency garnered the least submissions at just 7%, but recorded experiences under this area were spot on. It is clear that students are aware of the interconnectedness of organizations, and the following two excerpts show that they are reaching out to test their assumptions.

Excerpt 1

This year I was moved to a new position within the company. I am still an employee of the radiology facility, but I am contracted out to an orthopedic office to schedule MRIs and CTs. This is a different side of the office, and so I teamed up with the receptionist at the main office to organize that charting be done a little differently. I could see both sides of the business, and with this insight it is now a bit more streamlined.

Excerpt 2

I was given the opportunity to help implement a new testing method for detecting Strep. The process required me to perform a correlation between our method of collecting a throat culture, which took 48 hours to get results, and a new method which provided results in just five minutes. Once the study was completed, we were able to offer this improved method to our patients. The organization was willing to extend itself and seek improvements, and it was fascinating to be a part of this experiment. Now I feel better being able to provide data to physicians in a quick turnaround time.

Business Skills Competency: World Café Debrief

Throughout all three World Café sessions, the financial risk management sub-competency seemed to generate the most 3 × 5 cards. As shown in Table 8.1, communications and human resources/staffing issues were the next largest pool of "idea cards," and were fairly evenly represented. Customer satisfaction was listed as a final cluster of conversations under this competency.

Three streams of conversation transpired relevant to financial/ risk management. The first was safety focused, and terms like cybersecurity, safeguarding medical records, and quick thinking were used. Perhaps recent systems breaches reported in the media factored in, but there was a sense of urgency associated with this aspect of finance. Another thread was financial health of the institution, and terms like running lean departments, budget, and how to save money were applied. The third stream related to the mechanics of finances, such as planning, preparation, problem solving, and assessments.

Under communications and interpersonal skills, students voiced that knowledge of the job was equally as important as

Table 8.1 World Café Business Skills Competency Debrief

Customer Satisfaction	Human Resources	Financial/Risk Management	Communication/ Interpersonal Skills
• Access • Branding • Listening • Safety • Satisfaction survey	• Equality • Facebook/ social media monitor • Flexibility • Hiring/firing • People skills • Performance review • Recruitment • Resources • Scheduling • Staffing • Succession planning	• Assessment • Budget management • Cybersecurity • Documentation • How to run a "lean" department • How to save the organization money • Preparation • Problem solving • Reimbursement schedules • Risk management of medical records • Quick thinking • Safety strategy • Strategic planning	• Attitude • Both soft/hard skills • Common sense • Knowledge of job • Loyalty • Meeting deadlines • Multi-tasking • Networking with colleagues • Skills building • Teamwork • Time management • Writing skills

the soft skills. Terms like deadlines time management, writing skills, and common sense speak to the hard skills. Attitude, loyalty, teamwork, and networking with colleagues are also necessary business skills.

One card seemed to stand out under human resources; monitoring social media. The conversation explored an institution's purview to monitor an employee's Facebook page and somehow factor that information into performance reviews. Many felt strongly that this was not a fair policy. Some students mentioned that their social media was a component of the hiring process, while others acknowledged deactivating their accounts prior to a serious career search. Another somewhat outlier 3 × 5 card placed under the human resources banner was succession planning. Apparently one table had a robust dialogue on this subject, and it occurred during a joint session of students and healthcare professions. This exchange demonstrates that having a different perspective and voice at the table can broaden perspective.

Customer satisfaction was the fourth area under business competencies, and it was the least represented. Of course the satisfaction survey was listed on more than one 3 × 5 card, and perhaps this is because the most basic avenue to gauge whether or not the patient is pleased with their healthcare experience. Although the "branding card" may seem out of place under the patient banner, in this case it directly tied back to hospital mergers in our region. Students wondered how the incoming "brand" may influence patient/customer perception of care.

Business Skills: Promising Practices

Focus on the Patient

Business skills that can support a focus on the patient are welcome in healthcare, now more than ever. Moving beyond HCAHPS scores is a project out of the United Kingdom that encouraged storytelling by the patient. The idea behind "Care Opinion" is to gather patient narratives and apply lessons learned from the material in a transparent and respectful manner. An online platform allows for real-time access and response, comments can be collected and tagged into themes or trends, and data profiles about the number of hits, updates, or impacts of stories can be monitored. A variation on this application is happening in the United States as well.

"More than 100 large U.S. health systems are collecting and reporting patient reviews online...by 2013, 31 percent of Americans had read patients comments online and 21 percent used them when selecting a clinician" (Browne and Shaller 2018, p. 2). Healthcare workers have to be aware of options for patients to voice opinions and then appropriately apply and manage the collective conversation.

As empowering as storytelling is, there are other ways to elicit comments from patients. Patient satisfaction surveys, focus groups, and interviews come to mind. One institution applied a creative concept mapping approach to prompt insight into how to build patient trust. The idea of a concept map is to pose a central inquiry, such as "what builds institutional or patient/provider trust," and then document all contributing elements. Sometimes a concept map might appear as spokes on a wheel, or branches on a tree with the hub and trunk as the central point of inquiry. The group-generated concept map is further vetted into themes, discussed, and rendered down to key interlocking concepts that answer the inquiry. Findings from concept mapping with patients revealed that "local healthcare leaders seeking to build institutional trust should implement processes to improve protection of patient privacy, support patient-provider relationships, and engender respect for patients, and that they should develop system-led guidelines to support these principles" (Doty and Nelson 2018, p. E128). Going directly to the client for suggestion on how to improve the service environment and experience makes sense.

Innovation

Earlier in this chapter, AI was mentioned as a rapidly emerging technology. "AI has the potential to improve accuracy, precision, and timeliness of patient diagnosis, and 90% of U.S. hospitals and insurance companies will implement AI systems by 2025" (Copeland et al. 2014, p. 14). AI appears to be a promising practice that is here to stay. Another technology-based practice that is gaining in traction is point-of-care diagnostics (POC), which enable more convenient testing both inside and outside the traditional clinical setting. Given the preponderance of chronic conditions that require testing and monitoring, the POC is a timely idea. "POC will total nearly $3 billion in 2021, up from $2.13 billion in 2015" (Copeland et al. 2014, p. 18). AI and POC are new and innovative ideas, and have yet to be fully vetted for optimal potential and positioning in the healthcare system. But, it is unlikely that once novel ideas are shown to advance an agenda; they might instead be discarded.

A new role evolving right alongside technology is the Chief Innovation Officer (CIO). In order to ascertain the function of this new C-Suite position, a study of the 40 largest health systems by revenue across the United States were surveyed. Findings included: "structure and function of the chief innovation officer to be diverse across systems – 52 percent reported a strategic focus, 24 percent operational, and 24 percent financial" (Jain and Schulman 2018). These foci were further investigated to reveal a variety of mandates within the CIO wheelhouse.

Some hospitals outsourced innovation to consultant groups, while others established in-house incubators to test new projects and approaches to emergent challenges. An possible alternate CIO function was the pursuit of venture capital to support novel ideas. For the CIO to be successful, there has to be a direct link to the CEO and the board. A business model that supports innovation is also essential.

A third promising area of innovation comes from the AHA. The "AHA Innovation 90 Program" is both agile and adaptable, as it encourages teams to identify problems, propose solutions, and implement remedies all within a 90-day timeframe. The expedited process discourages the perfection paralysis that many new initiatives suffer from, and follows a rapid prototyping method; the idea is to pose a question and answer it.

The Carle Foundation Hospital in Urbana Illinois was curious about how millennials view healthcare from a payer/ insurer point of view. "According to the U.S. Census Bureau, sometime in 2019 the millennial generation – those born from 1981 to 1996 – will surpass baby boomers as the nation's largest population group, at 73 million strong" (Aliello 2018). Using a focus group method, the Carle team discovered a number of relevant insights into how the millennial target group approaches healthcare. As predicted, individuals in the group are internet wired and used apps for instant access to services. They did value healthcare and wellness programming. The proposed product at the end of the 90 days was a new health plan offering.

Overall the "AHA Innovation 90 Program" kept the team focused, enabled patient engagement, and identified a customizable product for a specific issue and audience.

Assessing Employee Values and Strengths

In order to fulfill any promising practice whether patient-centric or an innovative process or product, assessment of the healthcare workforce has merit. Two tried and true tools that readily come to mind are the Values in Action (VIA) Survey on Character Strengths and Virtues, and the CliftonStrengths Assessment.

The VIA derives from the seminal work of Dr. Martin Seligman from the University of Pennsylvania. Specializing in the field of positive psychology, Dr. Seligman documented a classification of 24 value-based strengths. A VIA Survey is available online for free with simple registration. "Knowing your character strengths isn't just interesting information. When skillfully applied, character strengths can actually have a significant positive impact on your life. Research shows that using your character strengths can help you: buffer against, manage and overcome problems, improve your relationships, enhance health and overall well-being" (VIA Institute on Character 2018). The intent in taking the VIA Survey is to become familiar with personal strengths and continue to strengthen the asset in daily functions. Starting with the natural and familiar is likely to encourage strength-based performance. This does not necessarily mean that a characteristic that is not as prominent is to be ignored; rather, there is increased contentment and improved commitment when values/ strengths and tasks are aligned.

The VIA Survey has been a beneficial tool in my academic classes when I encourage students to self-reflect and assess their inner core. The VIA scores foster talking points about emotional intelligence, the emotional competency framework, and "encourage the heart" from the leadership challenge. Students are also directed to incorporate their strengths into elevator speeches and personal branding.

The free and easy access to the VIA might be motivation enough for an institutional department without any training budget to consider its use. However, the value in the tool and potential applications far outshine simply a price point consideration. I have used the VIA alongside Appreciative Inquiry sessions in professional development workshops and with clients as a consultant.

A similar tool to the VIA is CliftonStrengths 34. The assessment was first published in 2001 by Don Clifton and Marcus Buckingham, and was quickly incorporated into performance assessments and workshops. There are 34 themes that assess individual traits and recommend how to build teams inclusive of a broad range of strengths. "Each CliftonStrengths theme sorts into one of four domains: strategic thinking, executing, influencing, and relationship building. These domains describe how people and teams use their talents to work with information, make things happen, influence others, and build relationships" (CliftonStrengths 34 2018). "Simply learning their strengths makes employees 7.8% more productive, and teams that focus on strengths every day have 12.5% greater productivity. What's more, nearly two-thirds (61%) of these employees were engaged, twice the average of U.S. workers" (Sorenson 2014).

Closing Thoughts

Business skill competencies are numerous and can be challenging, and not all employees might be well versed and capable in every aspect of operations. Placing business requirements in context of rapidly developing technology, consumer expectations, and employee values and strengths does provide a roadmap to take on the charge. The watchwords of adaptability and agility can best be applied to the work ahead for the healthcare workforce. Transitioning from medical records in tall stacks to electronic formats will seem like a mere inconvenience compared to daily interface with Artificial Intelligence and escalating point-of-care diagnostics. Providing opportunities for employees to acknowledge their strengths and interact with patients in their care in meaningful ways has the potential to offset the perception that machines rule. A balance between high tech and high touch will be needed.

References

Aliello, Carl. "Change Is on the Horizon: The Carle Foundation and its Health Plan Look to Engage Millennials in Their Health and Wellness." American Hospital Association. Accessed October 5, 2018. https://ahainnovation.org/wp-content/uploads/2018/05/carle-case-study.pdf

Browne, Katherine, and Shaller, Dale. 2018. "Tell Me a Story: How Patient Narrative Can Improve Health Care." *Robert Wood Johnson Foundation*, (May): 1–8. Accessed October 5, 2018. https://www.rwjf.org/content/dam/farm/reports/issue_briefs/2018/rwjf445525

CliftonStrengths 34. Accessed October 5, 2018. https://www.gallupstrengthscenter.com/home/en-us/cliftonstrengths-themes-domains

Copeland, Bill, Yaynor, Michael, and Shah, Sonal. 2014. "Top 10 Health Care Innovations: Achieving More for Less." Accessed October 5, 2018. https://www2.deloitte.com/us/en/pages/life-sciences-and-health-care/articles/top-10- health-care-innovations. html

Djukic, Jovanka. 2015. "Training to Increase Internal Mobility." *Talent Development*, 69(9): 8.

Doty, Amanda, and Nelson, Deborah. 2018. "Identification of Approaches to Improve Patient Trust in Health Systems: A Group Concept Mapping Study." *Journal of Healthcare Management*, 63(5): e116–e128.

General Dynamics Health Solutions. 2015. "Health Systems Find That Outsourcing IT Saves Money, Boosts Productivity, Improves Care." *Hospitals & Health Networks*: 89(10): 21.

Jain, Sheha, and Schulman, Kevin. 2018. "Committing To Transformation: Chief Innovation Officers and the Role of Organizational Redesign." *Health Affairs*, Accessed October 5, 2018. https://www.healthaffairs.org/do/10.1377/hblog20180920.793517/full/

Platonova, Elena, and Hernandez, Robert. 2013. "Innovative Human Resource Practices in U.S. Hospitals: An Empirical Study." *Journal of Healthcare Management*, 58(4): 290–301.

Puranik, Marty. 2018. "How Cloud Computing Meets Healthcare Needs." *Health Management Technology*, 39(2): 28.

Riggi, John. 2018. "What's Your Cyber Security Profile? 12 Considerations for CEOs." American Hospital Association. Accessed October 5, 2018. https://www.aha.org/system/files/2018-09/Whats_Your_Cyber_Risk_Profile_2.pdf

Roemer, Kurt. 2017. "Innovations for Healthcare that Ensure Patient Privacy, While Transforming Care Delivery." *Health Management Technology*, 38(10): 10.

Sorenson, Susan. 2014. "How Employees' Strengths Make Your Company Stronger." *Business Journal* (September). Accessed October 5, 2018. https://news.gallup.com/businessjournal/167462/employees-strengths-company-stronger.aspx

Thomas, Sarah. 2018. "Taking the Robot out of the Human: Meet the Health Care Workforce of the Future." Accessed October 5, 2018. https://www2.deloitte.com/us/en/pages/life-sciences-and-health-care/articles/health-care-current-may1-2018.html

VIA Institute on Character. 2018. Accessed October 5, 2018. https://www.viacharacter.org/www/Character-Strengths

Chapter 9

Healthcare Workforce Transitioning

Competencies and the Healthcare Workforce

An intent for this book has been to nudge a thought process on linkages between professional competencies and grooming a healthcare workforce in as much transition as our healthcare system while imagining potential in such a vision. By now, the reader has certainly come to realize that competencies are numerous and ever evolving to meet shifting and mounting demands. For example, chaos competency was introduced to address recent experiences as personnel respond to Ebola, SARS, or numerous natural disasters. In this chapter, career competencies are addressed, and yes, these are an acknowledged set of skills. It is challenging to isolate a grouping of competencies that seem able to serve as a framework for the complexity of today's healthcare system, and in turn the workforce who have to successfully navigate it.

Ability to Apply Competency

Five general and overarching competencies served as the foundation for an emergent curriculum in healthcare management: communication, leadership, professionalism, knowledge of the healthcare environment, and business skills. These same set of competencies were then translated into professional development experiences so that students could explore and learn lessons. Finally, dedicated competency conversations were held with students and healthcare practitioners to expand awareness about expectations and accountability. These activities have reinforced the concept that competencies are only worthwhile when applied.

The potential vision of a workforce that is agile, adaptable, and accountable rests with the knowledge that talent has to be exercised and channeled to the right task at the right time. That level of awareness is what Captain Sullenberger used when he landed an airplane on the Hudson River. It is reflective and grounded on lessons learned. As academics and caring healthcare professionals we have to think about how and where connections between learning and application can be made.

Academia's Role

Special skills that the healthcare workforce will require to be successful while on-the-job are fluctuating. With the aging population a focus on nursing homes and at-home caregivers is on the rise. Staff interacting with this geriatric population will have to be sensitized to the special needs and abilities of this audience. "Demand for registered nurses and certified nursing assistants is projected to grow faster than all other occupations over the next seven years – 16 percent for RNs and 18 percent for CNAs, compared to seven percent for all other jobs" (Kuhn 2017, p. 22). The Nicholas County Career and Technical Education Center in West Virginia provide real-life learning experiences for their RN and CNA students through a Geriatric Simulator suit. When students don the suit, they are able to mimic typical challenges of the target audience, such as hearing and vision loss and compromised motor skills. One key result is that the empathy level of the young students is increased, and this places both urgency and humanity on their learning. Building these vital connections into the learning experience will go a long way in putting the healthcare worker role into focus.

The National Association of Colleges and Employers (NACE) has identified a set of competencies that employers are seeking, and the list is not surprising. The competencies of Critical Thinking/Problem Solving, Oral/ Written Communications, Digital Technology, Leadership, Professionalism/Work Ethic, and Global/Intercultural Fluency were on the list. In general, employers tend to rate the students lower on competencies than the students themselves do. However, the National Association of Colleges and Employers (2018) report that the only competency in which "employers rated the proficiency of college graduates higher than did graduating seniors was digital technology. Employers also believe new hires are hitting the mark on teamwork; more than three-quarters related new graduates as proficient in this competency. Students agree, with 85 percent considering themselves proficient in teamwork."

One perhaps surprising competency that NACE has identified as needed for career readiness was Career Management. Preparation includes but is not limited to career basics like writing cover letters, crafting a resume, activating a LinkedIn account, and interview role-playing. Seeking opportunities to experience competencies such as the PDSL Portfolios, serving in student leadership roles, and participation in regional case competitions are equally beneficial. An institution's career center will be a tremendous asset in exposing students to career planning resources. For example, a requirement of so many position applications is exclusively through an online portal. Unless the candidate application or resume has specific terms, an algorithm will kick it out of contention. The resolution is for students to possess the requisite skills for a position, visualize themselves applying their trade, and also having the knowledge to gain entry into their discipline.

Challenging students to describe their ideal career and then charting a course to achieve the objective is an important responsibility of higher education. Starting with entry level courses I encourage students to think about their niche in the market. I have had several students who have laser focus on their specific "ideal" job. One student wanted to be a representative for the DaVinci robotic surgical arm. Every course assignment through research, marketing, quality improvement, and policy, she concentrated on DaVinci through the respective class lens. Another student was passionate about diabetes prevention and treatment, and he too tracked every course assignment through this subject. In essence, by the time of graduation, he was a subject matter expert (SME) in this topic. A culminating capstone course for him was obviously, and luckily realized; conducting a gap analysis of a regional diabetes coalition.

Organizational Roles

Just as academia must groom the healthcare workforce, so too do organizations have a responsibility to contribute. A study of two large institutions, Kaiser Permanente and Montefiore Health System, was conducted to ascertain models of workforce planning and development processes (WFPD). The inquiry focused on the skills necessary to enhance capacities of the workforce. A number of WFPD principles were identified that collectively address what an adaptive workforce might look like: "(1) situated in a set of core values contexts; (2) integrated both internally and externally; (3) focused on a whole-system perspective; (4) responsive to changing demand; (5) based on consensus building, that is (6) continuous; and (7) generative and requires real and continued investment" (Pittman and Scully-Russ 2016, p. 14).

These principles demonstrate the broad scope of actions necessary to nurture and sustain the workforce, and they have been profiled in this book. The good news is that examples do exist of an adaptive workforce. The American College of Physicians Foundation and the European Federation of Internal Medicine recommended systemic integration of core values on professionalism. The Ohio Hospital Association institutions profiled as environmental stewards are certainly honoring a whole-system perspective. The State of Washington is leading the way to a responsive and changing demand for at-home healthcare as the leader in training personal care aids. Care Opinion, a process that captures storytelling by patients, is an example of a generative approach to improving the patient experience. The public health accreditation process has taken core competencies and realized a continued investment in elevating quality in service delivery.

The healthcare enterprise is rapidly changing to mirror consumer demands and trends. With an incursion of technology, shifting financial structures, and simply the pace of the industry, the healthcare workforce is taxed. Forward-thinking strategies should be considered in order to counterbalance the weary workforce.

The first approach is an increased focus on collaboration. New team members, roles, responsibilities, and shared burden will likely make an overwhelming task appear more manageable. Organizations are exploring mergers with partners that can boost brand and expand services. With new partnerships come new team members, skill sets, and an infusion of creativity.

The second strategy is to "create policies and regular opportunities for the workforce to debrief, share stories about their experience of caregiving, and reflect on the impact of the work on their emotional and professional lives" (Levkovich 2016, p. 186). A number of institutions hold team huddles, which not only provides a venue for ongoing planning but also for expressing concerns about overall functions.

The third strategy is building trust within institutions through initiatives that are supportive of the workforce and their needs, and this can make a difference. One respected and inclusive initiative is the Baldridge process, which assesses seven elements across an institution. Notably, one of the key indicators is the workforce. "Baldridge winners typically provide 10 days of training per full-time equivalent worker per year, several times the traditional level – including protocols and other work processes, learning servant leadership, understanding performance measures – and negotiating improvement goals" (Griffith 2017, p. 334).

The role of the organization in nurturing the healthcare workforce cannot be understated. It is the very system that brings together teams of talented professionals and provides a platform upon which to perform optimally. Care has to be given to the environment, resources, processes, and protocols that enable high-level functioning to occur.

Fourth Aim: Focus on the Healthcare Workforce

The Triple Aim framework targeted improved patient care experiences, inclusive of quality, population health, and reduction in per capita healthcare cost. Since its launch in 2007 some progress has been made to achieve the Triple Aim objective. In order to advance the directive further, perhaps it is time to add another dimension and name: Quadruple, or Fourth Aim. The healthcare workforce would be the added attribute; the very entity charged with making patient engagement, population health, and cost containment a reality.

In striving for a more resilient workforce, it might be beneficial to first identify what is occurring in the field. Kreitzer (2015) said "Stress and burnout are very significant issues, characterized by loss of enthusiasm for work, feelings of cynicism, and low sense of personal accomplishment – only 30% of employees in the United States, and 13% across 142 countries feel engaged at work." Statistics like these give credence to the sentiment: "care of the patient requires care of the provider" (Kreitzer 2015, p. 3).

A study of registered nurses indicated that relational coordination (RC) is a worthy element of the Fourth Aim. Nurses are on the frontline of patient care and work as members of a complex team. It therefore makes sense that if RNs perceived better relational experiences and teamwork skills it would have positive implications for patient care. In fact, according to Havens et al. (2018, p. 133). "Building RC among those delivering care may improve well-being and the experience of providing care – it can improve provider outcomes in three ways by: (1) enhancing information processing; (2) changing emotional well-being; and (3) enabling resilient responses to performance pressures – cohesive work groups were associated with higher engagement."

Creating work environments that engage and sustain enthusiasm for one's professional calling is an attainable and necessary goal. In this era of staff shortages and increased demands, focus on the employee as the Fourth Aim makes sense.

Job Engagement and Satisfaction

One working concept of job engagement and job satisfaction included three essential characteristics: vigor, dedication, and absorption. "Vigor represents high levels of energy and resilience when working and can provide agencies with drive and problem solving capacities, dedication – level of enthusiasm and meaning derived from work, and absorption – capacity of practitioners to fully concentrate on their work and be immersed in their role" (Noblet et al. 2017, p. 244). Employees are more content and productive when they have an opportunity to exercise these three characteristics on the job. As vigor seems to be the opposite of burn out, it seems logical that engaging employees in meaningful work that is linked to organizational mission and vision would have a positive effect.

A national Public Health Workforce Interest and Needs Survey polled all state health agencies across the United States to ascertain a snapshot of job satisfaction. The findings from the survey seem to agree with recommended Fourth Aim strategies. Having a content workforce is important, especially under healthcare reform and the ACA where personnel will likely have to do more with fewer colleagues. According to the findings of the survey, the top contributors to job satisfaction were notable as "training, communication, creativity, workload, and whether individuals recommend their organization as a good place to work" (Harper et al. 2015, p. S52).

It is easy to see the connection between having training opportunities, communication, and creative outlets at work, as these experiences serve to enhance daily functions and responsibilities. Workload has to be perceived as equitable and balanced to add to job satisfaction. When teams share accountability for wrap-around patient service, a reasonable assumption can be made that the workload is less a burden than a choice.

Positioning an organization as a "good place to work" is a bit more nuanced. If the institution has a solid mission and vision statement with actions that back up the verbiage, it is a starting point. Leadership will have to clearly demonstrate how daily activities of each employee are needed in order to realize the organizational vision. Individual employees will then have to judge for themselves if dedication and reputation are sufficient to sustain a connection.

Whether it is called job satisfaction, well-being, or contentment, it is a logical point to consider if we are going to be successful in healthcare reform. Enactment of policies that address workforce well-being was the focus of a study by Schulte et al. (2016 p. E36), who identified four areas that contribute to a healthy workplace including "physical work environment, the psychological work environment, personal health resources in the workplace, and enterprise community involvement." The authors argue that unless the national conversation around these elements of job well-being are elevated to the policy level, improvements will not be realized.

Everyone enjoys a nice work environment, and the physical work space of many healthcare enterprises meet a reasonable standard. The environment is more than simply the space; it also entails access to tools and resources to accomplish requisite tasks while allowing ease of navigation and mission affinity. Psychological variables are more complex, and include fulfilling preferences and capabilities within one's role and responsibility as well as feelings of belonging. Closely aligned with psychological needs, personal health resources in the workplace include meeting safety requirements. Enterprise community involvement does seem to tie back to the earlier point of perceiving one's employer as a "good place to work." Does the employee see their institution as having a responsible presence, reputation, and brand in the community, and are they proud to be associated with it.

Given the high-stress and uncertain atmosphere that most healthcare delivery functions within, it seems that there would be a logical correlation between a more engaged employee and patient engagement. It is more critical than ever at this juncture to sustain the workforce. Against this backdrop, we need to frame career satisfaction as an investment. Akkermans and Tims (2017) pose two interlaced concepts for perceived career success: meaningfulness and work and person fit. Gauging significance of one's role and function in a particular setting is a real value. If disconnect exists between personal skills and preferences and the work we are required to do daily, it would not take long for job dissatisfaction to set in. The authors suggest three types of career competences that need to naturally occur for an employee to feel job satisfaction. "Reflective career competencies include reflection on motivation – values, passions, and innovations; communicative career competencies encompass networking, which pertains to – ability to expand this network for career-related purposes; and behavioral career competencies – exploration and searching for work-related career opportunities" (Akkermans and Tims 2017, p. 173). One approach to exercising these three competencies in order for the healthcare workforce to feel more in control of their careers is through job crafting.

Job Crafting

The idea of job crafting may strike apprehension into the hearts of some managers because there is an element of the uncertain about it. There is also a sense of loss of control in an already potentially chaotic atmosphere. "Job crafting focuses on the process by which employees change elements of their jobs and relationships with others to redefine the meaning of their work and the social environment at work – insights into and awareness of job demands and resources stimulates adjustments in work" (Van Wingerden 2016, p. 58). The locus of control does seem to be on the employee but with stellar communication built on trust, managers can encourage job crafting.

One example of job crafting is job sharing. Two colleagues working full-time and feeling overwhelmed might approach their supervisor to explore the possibility of each working part-time. Position consolidation is another option. Perhaps a former volunteer coordinator moved into a foundation officer role might find a way to either combine the two functions or mentor her replacement. Millennials would likely craft their ideal position as remote or off-site work and tethered to technology. Employees feeling a bit isolated from a team,could suggest weekly huddles to satisfy their need for the big picture. The list is endless and based on personal and organizational needs.

Organizations contemplating incorporation of job crafting into their enterprise would have to consider their best approach. "Job crafting is comprised of (at least) three work strategies (1) seeking challenges – creating novel and useful ideas, products, services, organizational processes, (2) seeking resources – asking for feedback/support, and (3) reducing (hindering) demands – asking a colleague to cover a work shift" (Gordon et al. 2015, p. 194). Leaders would have to ask which of these strategies is feasible. Resources perhaps are already stretched thin and staffing is currently creatively implemented, and so fostering innovation might be a good fit.

The onus for crafting toward job satisfaction does not reside solely with the organization; individuals must also take accountability for their career. To model this point, I have incorporated job crafting as a class assignment within one course in our healthcare management program. Once students conduct their personal Values in Action Survey of Strengths and document their personal profile, they are challenged to explore a potentially compatible corporate culture that would likely match their self-analysis. The students conduct an environmental scan of potential employers in the Treasure Coast region or the location of their career aspiration. They are instructed to consider each sector of the enterprise; hospitals, clinics, profit and non-profit organizations, institutes, and government. The mission statements of organizations are taken into consideration, their annual reports, how they craft their position descriptions, and when possible, personal interviews with prospective colleagues. Additional corresponding elements to consider include patterns of communication, interactions, attitudes, corporate self-image, physical environment, former employees, and self-assessments.

There are a number of ways to craft or enrich the experience once on the job. One approach is clarification of job tasks or functions, viewing these actions against the bigger backdrop of the mission of the organization and realizing that everyone's efforts count. Another effort is to broaden relationships through participation on workgroups, mentoring, or volunteering in an area of interest. Perception is another, and perhaps the most powerful of job crafting tactics. Framing the nature of one's work is a vital component of job satisfaction. For example, a hospital custodian is actually responsible for infection control, a volunteer coordinator is a conduit for human resources, and the dietary aid is contributing to nutrition and improved health. How we think about our jobs helps to craft improvements.

Closing Thoughts: Keeping the Conversation Alive

The World Café experience has greatly added to understanding the connection between competency and expectations for accountabilities in a health career. Students and healthcare professionals alike both discovered something special about each other through simply posing questions and listening to the response.

In fact, The World Café initiative has been as so rewarding that I have incorporated it into the capstone course, which is the culminating experience for students prior to graduation. Once each semester, a modified World Café is facilitated to foster conversation about regional healthcare trends, introduce potential employers to our students, and for students to network with future colleagues. The energy in the room is palpable, and the outcomes can only be beneficial for all participants.

As an extension of the World Café, healthcare professionals have become mentors. If a partner agency is presenting findings of an ongoing protocol, hosting a focus group, or presenting an annual report, an invitation is extended to our students. Our Health Professional Mentors provide avenues for students to job shadow, which is a short-term opportunity unlike a semester-long internship. These intermittent experiences appear to meet the busy schedules of healthcare executives who want to mentor students but have limited time on their calendars.

Healthcare management competencies were the focus of our World Café experience, and we concentrated on just five broad skills. We posed the inquiry about how students might seek experiences in each of the competencies, and what lessons they learn from such encounters. Competencies provide an important benchmark for skills, knowledge, behaviors, and attitudes that one must possess to be successful on the job, and making that connection is vital.

The healthcare workforce is such an essential asset to our healthcare reform objective that more attention has to be paid to this resource. The idea of the Fourth Aim is mainly interesting because it shines the light on the connection between meeting the Triple Aim through acknowledgment of the role of the workforce.

My hope is that the conversation about the healthcare workforce in transition may continue, and that we apply competencies in some form as our coalescing beacon.

References

Akkermans, Jos, and Tims, Maria. 2017. "Crafting Your Career: How Career Competencies Relate to Career Success via Job Crafting." *Applied Psychology: An International Review*, 66(1): 168–195.

Gordon, Heather, Demerouti, Evangelia, LeBlac, Pascale, and Bipp, Taja. 2015. "Job Crafting and Performance of Dutch and American Health Care Professionals." *Journal of Personal Psychology*, 14(4): 192–202.

Griffith, John. 2017. "An Organizational Model for Excellence in Healthcare Delivery: Evidence from Winners of the Baldridge Quality Award." *Journal of Healthcare Management*, 62(5): 328–341.

Harper, E., Castrucci, N., Bhartapudi, K. 2015. "Job Satisfaction: A Critical, Understudied Facet of Workforce Development in Public Health." *Journal of Public Health Management and Practice*, 21(6 Supp.): S46–S55.

Havens, Donna, Gittell, Jody, and Vasey, Joseph. 2018. "Impact of Relational Coordination on Nurse Job Satisfaction, Work Engagement and Burnout." *Journal of Nursing Administration*, 48(3): 132–140.

Kreitzer, Mary Jo. 2015. "The Wellbeing of the Workforce in Healthcare and Beyond." *Global Advances in Health and Medicine Journal*, 4(5): 3–4.

Kuhn, Emily. 2017. "Teaching In-Demand Skills: How Healthcare Educators Engage Today's Students." *Techniques: Connecting Education and Careers*, 92(7): 18–23.

Levkovich, Natalie. 2016. "The Fourth Aim: How Do We Care for Our Healthcare Workforce?." *Families, Systems, and Health*, 34(2): 185–186.

National Association of Colleges and Employers. 2018. "Are College Graduates Career-Ready?" Accessed October 13, 2018. http://www.naceweb.org/career-readiness/competencies/are-college-graduates-career-ready/

Noblet, Andrew, Allisey, Amanda, Nielson, Ingrid, Cotton, Stacey, LaMontagne, Anthony, and Page, Kathryn. 2017. "The Work-Based Predictors of Job Engagement and Job Satisfaction Experienced by Community Health Professionals." *Healthcare Management Review*, 42(3): 237–246.

Pittman, Patricia, and Scully-Russ, Ellen. 2016. "Workforce Planning and Development in Times of Delivery System Transformation." *Human Resources for Health*, 1–15.

Schulte, Paul, Guerin, Rebecca, Schill, Anita, Bhattacharya, Anasua, Cunningnham, Thomas, Pandalia, Sudha, Eggert, Donald, and Stephenson, Carol. 2015. "Considerations for Incorporating Well-Being in Public Policy for Workers and Workplaces." *American Journal of Public Health*, 105(8): 31–44.

Van Wingerden, Jessica. 2016. "Job Crafting in Organizations: What Can It Mean for Your Workplace." *Leader to Leader*, 81(Summer): 58–59.

Index

A

ACHE, *see* American College of Healthcare Executives
Agility, 135
AHA, *see* American Hospital Association
AI, *see* Appreciative Inquiry; Artificial intelligence
AIDET (Acknowledge, Introduce, Duration, Explanation, and Thank You), 69
American College of Healthcare Executives (ACHE), 26
American Hospital Association (AHA), 135; *see also* Business skills competency
AHA Innovation 90 Program, 148–149
Appreciative Inquiry (AI), 93; *see also* Healthcare leadership competency
affirmative principles into leadership development program, 96
BEST Initative, 95
Ds associated with, 93
LDS course design, 94

Leadership Practices Inventory, 95
Protocol, 12
Artificial intelligence (AI), 134, 147

B

BATHE (Background, Affect, Trouble, Handling, and Empathy/Exit), 76; *see also* Healthcare communication competency
Behavioral career competencies, 162
BEST Initative (the best Budget, patient Experience, Safety, Team), 95
Better Understanding and Learning Design Survey (BUILD Survey), 9; *see also* Healthcare competencies
focus group, 10–12
Student Listening Session, 12–13
BUILD Survey, *see* Better Understanding and Learning Design Survey
Business skills competency, 133, 151; *see also* Professional Development Service Learning

Business skills competency
(*Continued*)
agile and adaptable, 133
AHA Innovation 90 Program,
148–149
Chief Innovation Officer, 148
CliftonStrengths, 34, 150
concept map, 147
employee value and strength
assessment, 149–151
financial management, 139
focus on patient, 146–147
general management, 138
human resources, 135–136
human resources management,
140–141
information management,
141–142
innovation, 147–149
organizational dynamics,
143–144
PDSL insights, 137
point-of-care diagnostics, 148
promising practices, 146
quality improvement, 137–138
risk management, 139, 144
strategic planning and
marketing, 142–143
technology, 133–135
World Café debrief, 144–146

C

Career Professional Development
(CPD), 19; *see also*
Professional development
portfolios
practices, 20
Career readiness activities, 110;
see also Healthcare
professionalism
competency

Care management workers, *see*
Community health
workers
Care Opinion, 157
Carle Foundation Hospital, 149
Case Competition, 110–111; *see also*
Healthcare professionalism
competency
CBOs, *see* Community-based
organizations
Chasm report, 2; *see also*
Healthcare competencies
Chief Innovation Officer (CIO), 148;
see also Business skills
competency
CIO, *see* Chief Innovation Officer
CliftonStrengths, 34, 150; *see also*
Business skills competency
CLO, *see* Course Learning Outcome
Communicative career
competencies, 161
Community-based organizations
(CBOs), 21
Community health workers,
118; *see also* Healthcare
environment competency
Competencies, 5
Competency framework for
academic program,
8–9; *see also* Healthcare
competencies
Concept map, 147
Course Learning Outcome (CLO), 15
CPD, *see* Career Professional
Development

E

Emotional intelligence (EI), 89, 108
Engagement workers, *see* Community
health workers
E-professionalism, 108

F

Foundation for Medical
Excellence, 99
Fourth Aim, 158–159

G

Glenrose Rehabilitation Hospital, 80
Green Team, 128

H

HCAPHS, *see* Hospital Consumer
Assessment of Healthcare
Providers and Systems
Healthcare
enterprise, 157
field, 4
Healthcare communication
competency, 63, 77–78
BATHE, 76
Commit to Sit initiative, 76
communication skills, 68–69
consumer assessment of
healthcare providers and
systems, 75–77
facilitation and negotiation, 69–71
HCAPHS, 75
impact on six aims for quality
improvement, 63–66
IPPS, 76
linking communication skills to
six aims, 65
PDSL insights, 66–67
promising practices, 74
REDE model, 74–75
relationship management,
67–68
sandwich effect, 71–73
six aims for improvement, 63–65
World Café debrief, 71–74

Healthcare competencies, 1
Chasm report, 2
competency framework for
academic program, 8–9
development of healthcare
degree matrix, 13
healthcare competency potential,
4–8
implications for healthcare
workforce transitioning, 3–4
Institute of Medicine reports, 1–3
origin of competency
conversation, 1
value-based models, 2–3
Healthcare competency potential,
4; *see also* Healthcare
competencies
accreditation program
component, 8
areas in need of competency
development, 5
competency inspired initiative,
7–8
connection competencies, 6
public health and competencies, 6
Healthcare degree matrix
development, 13; *see also*
Healthcare competencies
course assessment methods, 16
course learning outcomes, 15
documentation of course
identifiers, 15
healthcare management
competencies, 13
key performance indicators, 15
program learning outcomes,
14–15
Healthcare environment
competency, 115,
130–131
changing healthcare workforce,
118–119

Healthcare environment
competency (*Continued*)
community and environment,
123–124
community health workers, 118
environmental stewardship,
127–128
Green Team, 128
healthcare environment
promising practices, 127
healthcare personnel, 121–123
healthcare systems and
organizations, 124–125
mirroring societal trends, 115
patient's perspective, 119–121
PDSL insights, 119
preparedness planning, 128–129
reinventing careers, 129–130
retailing of healthcare, 116–118
virtual healthcare, 116
virtual resources, 115
World Café debrief, 125–127
World Café Healthcare
Environment Competency
Debrief, 126
Healthcare Leadership Alliance
(HLA), 4
Healthcare leadership competency,
79, 96
Appreciative Inquiry, 93–96
assuming accountability, 79–81
communicating vision, 84–85
customized programs, 92–93
four themes emerging from
interviews, 80
guiding organization toward
success, 90–91
ICARE, 79
Institute for Healthcare
Improvement, 91–92
leadership development, 91
leadership skills, 81–82
managing change, 86–88

mentorship program for
emerging leaders, 80
organizational climate and
culture, 83–84
PDSL insights, 81
relating to people, 89–90
sub-competencies, 81
values-driven leadership skills, 88
World Café debrief, 88
World Café Leadership
Competency Debrief, 89
Healthcare professionalism
competency, 99, 112–113
accountability, 102–104
career readiness activities, 110
Case Competition approach,
110–111
for community and profession,
105–106
community partnerships, 100–101
countermeasure to ineffective
practices, 109
emotional intelligence, 108
E-professionalism, 108
institutional values and
professionalism, 112
Memphis Healthy U, 110
organizational culture, 100
PDSL insights, 102
pre-career professionalism
training, 109–110
professional development and
learning, 104–105
beyond professionalism toward
interprofessionalism,
99–102
promising training practices, 109
three program approach to
fostering professionalism, 110
Training Partnership for personal
care aides, 111–112
views of professionalism, 101
World Café debrief, 106–109

World Café Professionalism
    Competency Debrief, 107
Healthcare workforce, 133; *see also*
    Business skills competency
Healthcare workforce transitioning,
    1, 153, 164–165; *see also*
    Healthcare competencies
ability to apply competency,
    153–154
academia's role, 154–156
behavioral career
    competencies, 162
Care Opinion, 157
communicative career
    competencies, 161
competencies and healthcare
    workforce, 153
core competencies of successful
    healthcare executive, 3
forward-thinking strategies,
    157–158
Fourth Aim, 158–159
healthcare enterprise, 157
implications for, 3–4
job crafting, 162–164
job engagement and satisfaction,
    159–162
organizational roles, 156–158
overarching competencies,
    153–154
reflective career competencies, 161
Triple Aim framework, 158
WFPD principles, 156
Health Information Systems (HIS), 15
Health Professions Council
    (HPC), 101
HIS, *see* Health Information Systems
HLA, *see* Healthcare Leadership
    Alliance
Hospital Consumer Assessment of
    Healthcare Providers and
    Systems (HCAPHS), 75
HPC, *see* Health Professions Council

Human resources, 135–136;
    see also Business skills
    competency
management, 140–141

I

ICARE (Integrity, Commitment,
    Advocacy, Respect, and
    Excellence), 79; *see also*
    Healthcare leadership
    competency
IHI, *see* Institute for Healthcare
    Improvement
Inpatient Prospective Payment
    System (IPPS), 76
Insightful Practice, 34; *see also*
    Professional development
    portfolios
Institute for Healthcare
    Improvement (IHI), 91
Institute of Medicine reports, 1–3
Intelligent cognitive automation, 134
IPPS, *see* Inpatient Prospective
    Payment System

J

Jobs
    crafting, 162–164
    engagement and satisfaction, 159

K

Key Performance Indicators (KPIs), 15
KPIs, *see* Key Performance
    Indicators

L

Leadership Development Series
    (LDS), 94
Leadership Practices Inventory
    (LPI), 95

M

Machine learning, 134
Memphis Healthy U, 110; *see also*
    Healthcare professionalism
    competency
Mentorship program for emerging
    leaders, 80; *see also*
    Healthcare leadership
    competency

N

NACE, *see* National Association of
    Colleges and Employers
National Academy of Medicine, 5
National Association of Colleges
    and Employers (NACE), 155
Nicholas County Career and Technical
    Education Center, 154

O

Organizational culture, 100
Organizational Professionalism
    Charter Project, 99
Outreach workers, *see* Community
    health workers

P

Patient Protection and Affordable
    Care Act of 2010, 2
PCAs, *see* Personal care aides
PDSL, *see* Professional Development
    Service Learning
Personal care aides (PCAs), 111;
    see also Healthcare
    professionalism
    competency
PHAB, *see* Public Health
    Accreditation Board
PHF, *see* Public Health Foundation

Physical therapist assistant (PTA), 82
POC, *see* Point-of-care diagnostics
Point-of-care diagnostics (POC),
    148; *see also* Business skills
    competency
Portfolios, 20; *see also* Professional
    development portfolios
Professional development
    portfolios, 19, 35–36
    academic professional
      development process, 22
    advancing the institution, 34–35
    career advancement through,
      19–22
    Insightful Practice, 34
    personal career transitioning,
      32–34
Professional Development Service
    Learning (PDSL), 23,
    77–78; *see also* World Café
    Conversation
    applications, 29–32
    co-curricular, 39, 71
    for documenting interpretation
      of competencies, 42
    financial management, 139–140
    human resources
      management, 140
    information management, 141
    insights, 66–67, 81, 102, 119, 137
    learn more, and study
      beyond, 104
    portfolio, 22–25
    portfolio benefits, 32, 35
    portfolio initiative, 59
    to provide forum, 74
    reports, 25–29
    risk management, 139
    strategic planning submissions, 142
    submissions, 83, 84–85, 86, 91,
      119–121, 124, 138
    Survey Monkey form, 24

PTA, *see* Physical therapist
  assistant
Public Health Accreditation Board
  (PHAB), 7
Public Health Foundation
  (PHF), 6

Q

QI, *see* Quality improvement
Quadruple, *see* Fourth Aim
Quality improvement (QI), 137

R

RC, *see* Relational coordination
REDE model (Relationship,
  Establishment,
  Development, and
  Engagement model),
  74–75; *see also* Healthcare
  communication
  competency
Reflective career competencies, 161
Relational coordination (RC), 159
Robotic process automation, 134

S

Sandwich effect, 71–73; *see also*
  Healthcare communication
  competency
Service learning, 20–21; *see also*
  Professional development
  portfolios
Seven principles of World Café, 40;
  see also World Café
Six aims for improvement, 63;
  see also Healthcare
  communication
  competency
  effectiveness, 64

efficiency, 65
equity, 65
patient-centeredness, 64
safety, 63–64
timeliness, 64–65
SME, *see* Subject matter expert
Social media, 44
Standard healthcare job
  descriptions, 115; *see also*
  Healthcare environment
  competency
Student Listening Session,
  12–13; *see also* Better
  Understanding and
  Learning Design
Subject matter expert
  (SME), 156

T

Technology, 133; *see also* Business
  skills competency
cloud computing, 135
cybersecurity focus, 134
types of, 134
Training Partnership for personal
  care aides, 111–112; *see also*
  Healthcare professionalism
  competency
Triple Aim framework, 158

V

Values in Action Survey (VIA
  Survey), 149–150;
  see also Business skills
  competency
VIA Survey, *see* Values in Action
  Survey
Virtual resources, 115; *see also*
  Healthcare environment
  competency

W

WFPD, *see* Workforce planning and development processes
Workforce planning and development processes (WFPD), 156
World Café Communication Competency Debrief, 71, 72
World Café Conversation, 39–40, 43, 47–52, 58; *see also* Professional Development Service Learning
  connecting diverse perspectives, 45
  creating hospitable space, 42
  encouraging everyone's contribution, 44
  exploring questions that matter, 42–44
  healthcare-focused, 59–61
  ideal host, 46–47
  listening together for insight, 45
  purpose and context, 40
  questions, 43
  Scottish Health Council, 60
  seven principles, 40
  sharing collective discoveries, 45–46
  table host roles, 47–50
  training agenda, 49
World Café hosting, 50
  conversations, 54, 57–58
  debriefing, 54
  establishing agenda, 51–52
  facilitation steps, 52–54
  feedbacks, 55–57
  healthcare partner comments, 58
  inviting participants, 50
  lessons learned, 58–59
  venue and setting, 50–51

Printed in the United States
by Baker & Taylor Publisher Services